ALL-TIME GREAT
AFGHANS

ALL-TIME GREAT AFGHANS

50 Projects to Crochet and Knit

From McCall's Needlework & Crafts

MEREDITH® **PRESS**

New York

For **Meredith**® **Press**

Director: Elizabeth P. Rice
Editorial Project Manager: Susan A. Siegler
Project Editor: Veronica F. Towers
Production Manager: Bill Rose
Designer: H. Roberts

Distributed by Meredith Corporation, Des Moines, Iowa.

ISBN 0-696-02370-9
Library of Congress Catalog Card Number: 91-67782
Printed in Singapore

10 9 8 7 6 5 4 3 2 1

CONTENTS

Including degree of difficulty, technique, and portability.

9   INTRODUCTION

13 DESIGNER ACCENTS

14   BASKETWEAVE FLORAL COVERLET
Project for experienced crocheters.

19   PLAID COVERLET
Good beginner project for crocheters.

20   TWO-TONE CHECK
Project for beginning knitters.

21   TULIP PATCH
Easy and portable projects for crocheters.

25   FROM MY GARDEN
Portable project for crocheters with some experience.

29   FLOWER DIAMONDS
Portable project for crocheters with some experience.

33   NOSEGAYS FOR SPRING
Portable project for crocheters with some experience.

37   GERANIUM
Portable projects for crocheters with some experience.

41   MIDNIGHT MAGIC
Portable project for crocheters with some experience.

44   QUILT CHECK
Portable projects for crocheters with some experience.

49   HARVEST GLOW
Portable project for experienced crocheters.

53 LACY AND LUXURIOUS

54 ROSE PETALS WITH WHITE BLOSSOMS
For crocheters with some experience.

55 PEACH FLUFF
For crocheters with some experience.

59 FANCIFUL FLOWERS
Good scrap project for crocheters with some experience.

63 BLUE CABLES
Portable project for knitters with some experience.

64 GOLDEN BELLS
Textured project for knitters with some experience.

67 COZY BOW COVERLET
Easy and portable project for crocheters.

69 FLORAL CABLE
Project for knitters with some experience.

73 COUNTRY CASUAL

74 FLOWER BASKETS
Portable project for knitters with some experience.

77 BRICK-WASHED ARGYLE
Easy and portable project for crocheters.

79 FOLK-ART TREE
Project for experienced crocheters.

82 QUICK-CROCHET GRANNY
Easy and portable project for crocheters.

84 COLORGLOW
Project for crocheters with some experience.

86 CORNER TO CORNER
Easy project for beginning knitters.

89 COZY ARAN
Project for experienced knitters.

91 OCTAGON MOSAIC
Portable projects for crocheters with some experience.

95 PINWHEELS
Project for knitters with some experience.

Contents

99 PATTERNS WITH PIZAZZ

100 ADD A STRIP
Easy and portable project for crocheters.

102 COLOR-CHROME WIDE STEPS
Good scrap project for crocheters with some experience.

105 COLOR-CHROME NARROW STEPS
Good scrap project for crocheters with some experience.

108 PICNIC PLAID
Easy project for crocheters.

110 LOG CABIN
Portable project for knitters with some experience.

113 BLUE STAR "QUILT"
Exquisite project for experienced crocheters.

116 SUNSET RIPPLE
Easy project for crocheters.

119 GIRLS, BOYS, BABY'S TOYS

120 CANDY-STRIPE RIBBONS AND BOWS
Portable and easy projects for crocheters.

123 HATS AND MITTENS
Portable project for crocheters with some experience.

127 CARROUSEL HORSES
Project for crocheters with some experience.

129 QUICK-CROCHET CARRIAGE COVER
Fast, easy, and portable project for crocheters.

131 BABY GRANNY
Portable project for crocheters with some experience.

133 BABY ROSE
Project for experienced crocheters.

136 BABY QUILT AND PILLOW
Easy and portable projects for beginning crocheters.

139 SWEET DREAMS
Projects for crocheters with some experience.

143 CRAYON BOX
Easy and portable project for beginning crocheters.

147 WARM AND WINTRY

148 HOLLY ARAN
Project for knitters with some experience.

150 POINSETTIA BEDSPREAD
Portable project for crocheters with some experience.

155 WINTER WONDERLAND
Double-knit project for experienced knitters.

159 LUMBERJACK PLAID WITH POLAR BEARS
Easy project for knitters.

161 SNOWFIRE
Portable project for experienced crocheters.

165 SNOW CRYSTALS
Project for knitters with some experience.

171 CRISSCROSS CROCHET
Textured pattern for experienced crocheters.

173 AFGHAN BASICS

174 CROCHET

177 AFGHAN STITCH

179 KNITTING

184 EMBROIDERY STITCHES

185 GENERAL DIRECTIONS FOR CROCHETERS AND KNITTERS

191 INDEX

INTRODUCTION

The word afghan is derived from Afghanistan, a country in western Asia. Exactly why the word has been used for the knitted and crocheted coverlets so popular in America is really not known. But for almost a century and a half these handmade coverlets, used as throws, sofa coverings, extra blankets and carriage robes, have been called "afghans" by Americans.

Afghanistan has always been noted for its woven carpets, which feature geometric patterns in a myriad of vibrant colors. These carpets were exceedingly popular in America during the Victorian period. Perhaps American women in an effort to duplicate the intriguing squares, circles, stripes and zigzag effects of those brilliant carpets, created their own versions as lap rugs or "afghans" in knitting and crochet.

No matter how the term originated, we can be eternally grateful to the resourceful, imaginative, and skilled women who introduced the afghan. They've produced a wealth of patterns which have enriched our homes and our lives.

The collection of afghans in this book is a celebration of that American ingenuity. To reproduce them in the fabulous colors in which they are shown—just follow the step-by-step instructions provided with each project. Or, bring your own ingenuity into play by experimenting with yarn colors and textures to create adaptations of your very own!

Fifty Afghan Designs for Crocheters and Knitters

DESIGNER ACCENTS

Draped over a chair, the back of a sofa, or a settee, these afghans are certain to become the focal point of any room. The patterns are chosen to enhance the decor of your home, and each afghan is designed to suit many tastes and to be attractive in a variety of settings. Choose among several floral motifs, such as Tulip Patch—sure to add springtime freshness year-round—or the lovely, heirloom-quality Basketweave Floral Coverlet. In a totally different mode, the contemporary knit Two-Tone Check is great looking and easily worked in a simple stockinette stitch. For traditional tastes there is Harvest Glow, worked in rich autumn tones and crocheted "cables." And for crocheters who love popcorns and bobbles, Flower Diamonds is a sheer delight.

opposite page: *Basketweave Floral Coverlet*

BASKETWEAVE FLORAL COVERLET

Basketweave panels provide a delicate frame for this sophisticated floral sampler, certain to become a family heirloom. The motifs are embroidered in cross-stitch on an afghan-stitch background.

For how-to information, see Afghan Basics at the back of the book.

SIZE:
50" × 62"

MATERIALS:
Worsted-weight acrylic yarn (such as Brunswick Windrush): 17½ oz. Ecru; 7 oz. each Light Mauve Heather (A) and Light Strawberry Pink (B); 3½ oz. each Light Blue-Green (C), Medium Blue Heather (D), Medium Goldenrod (E), Blackberry Heather (F), Pale Pink (G), Deep Mauve Heather (I), Teal (J), Amethyst Heather (K), and Raspberry (L). Crochet hook size H (5 mm), or size required to obtain correct gauge. Tapestry needle. Yarn or thread for markers.

GAUGE:
16 sts = 4"; 20 rows = 4" (afghan st).

AFGHAN STITCH:
Ch desired number of sts.

Row 1: Insert hook in top lp only of 2nd ch from hook, draw up a lp, * insert hook in top lp of next ch, draw up a lp; repeat from * across.

Row 2: Yo and draw through 1 lp on hook, * yo and draw through 2 lps on hook; repeat from * across until 1 lp remains on hook.

Row 3: Sk first vertical bar, * insert hook under next vertical bar, yo and draw up a lp, repeat from * across.

Row 4: Repeat row 2. Repeat rows 3 and 4 for afghan st.

AFGHAN:
With Ecru, ch 251 loosely. Work row 1 of afghan stitch—250 lps. Work rows 2, 3, and 4 of afghan stitch. Repeat rows 3 and 4 until 249 rows have been completed. Do not end off.

EDGING: Rnd 1: With right side facing, ch 1, sc in each vertical bar across upper and lower edge, and between rows on each side of afghan, working 2 sc in each corner. Sl st in first sc to join.

Rnd 2: Ch 1, sc in joining, * ch 3, sk 2 sc, sc in next sc, repeat from * around. End sl st in first sc and ch-3 lp.

Rnd 3: Ch 1, sc in same ch-3 lp, * ch 3, sl st in next ch-3 lp, repeat from * around, working (sl st, ch 3, sl st) in each corner ch-3 lp. Sl st in first sl st to join. End off.

EMBROIDERY: Mark 10 rows from upper and lower edge, and 10 sts from each side (or outline entire area to be embroidered with long basting stitches). The cross-stitches are worked in the holes on each side of each vertical bar. Each square represents one cross-stitch in the color denoted by a symbol. Diagram indicates outline of each ribbon to be worked in A and B within marked area on afghan, as well as placement of numbered patterns. Work corresponding pattern in each numbered area of diagram. One full repeat is given for each pattern; repeat as many times as necessary in each section.

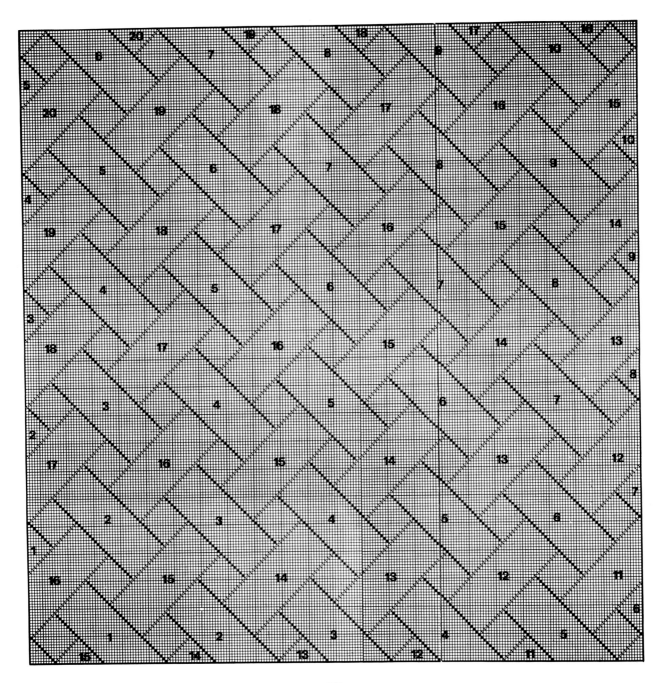

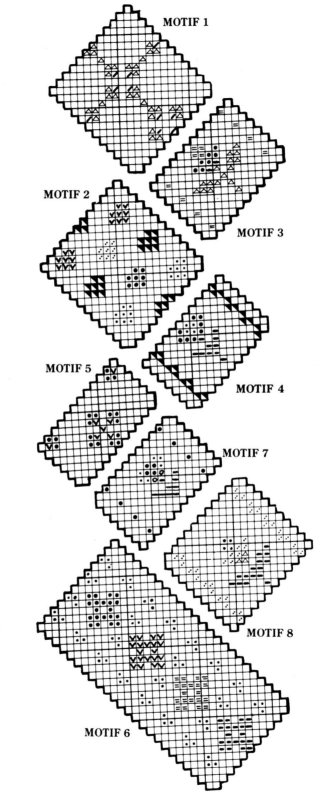

MOTIF 1

MOTIF 2

MOTIF 3

MOTIF 5

MOTIF 4

MOTIF 7

MOTIF 8

MOTIF 6

COLOR KEY

A •
B /
C △
D V
E •
F ◣
G ∴
I =
J ⊟
K ◎
L ✕

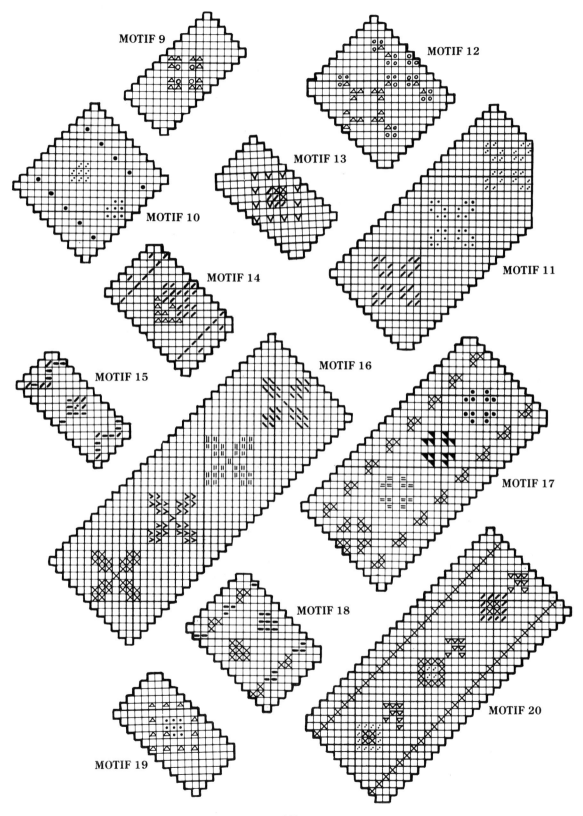

PLAID COVERLET

Crochet bold stripes, then cross them with strands of yarn woven in to create a sensational plaid coverlet—one that is suited to any decorating style.

For how-to information, see Afghan Basics at the back of the book.

SIZE:
39″ × 55″, plus fringe

MATERIALS:
Worsted-weight mohair: 8¾ oz. Lavender (A); 7 oz. each Red (B), Teal (C), and Burgundy (D). Crochet hook size G (4.25 mm) or size required to obtain correct gauge.

GAUGE:
18 sts = 4″; 16 rows = 4″.

PATTERN STITCH:
Row 1: Sc in 2nd ch from hook, * sc in next ch, ch 1, skip 1 ch, repeat from * across, end sc in last ch. Ch 1, turn each row.

Row 2: Sc in first sc, * sc in next ch-1 sp, ch 1, repeat from * across, end sc in next ch-1 sp, sc in last sc.

Row 3: Sc in first sc, * ch 1, sc in next ch-1 sp, repeat from * across, end ch 1, sc in last sc. Repeat rows 2 and 3 for pat st.

AFGHAN:
With A, ch 182. Work in pat st as follows:

Stripe 1: 6 rows A, 2 rows D, 6 rows A.
Stripe 2: 6 rows B, 2 rows A, 6 rows B.
Stripe 3: 6 rows C, 2 rows B, 6 rows C.
Stripe 4: 6 rows D, 2 rows C, 6 rows D. Repeat stripes 1–4 three times, end with stripe 1. End off.

FINISHING:
Cut 62″ lengths of yarn as follows: 24 A, 8 B, 16 C, 12 D. Beginning at bottom 1½″ from right side edge, weave 3 stripes (use 4 strands for each stripe) ½″ apart, make each st 2 rows high, (skip 6½″, work 3 stripes) four times. Work color sequence as follows: (ADA, CBC) twice, and ADA. Leave a 4″ length of yarn at each end for fringe.

FRINGE: Cut about 212 8″ lengths of A. Knot 2 strands every ½″ along top and bottom edges.

Plaid Coverlet (left); Two-Tone Check (right).

TWO-TONE CHECK

Knitters will enjoy the easy stitchery and fancy color changes needed to create this handsome windowpane check.

For how-to information, see Afghan Basics at the back of the book.

SIZE:
54" × 65"

MATERIALS:
Worsted-weight brushed acrylic/wool blend (such as Reynolds Kitten): 17½ oz. Dark Green (A); 3½ oz. each Magenta (B) and Rose (C). Knitting needles No. 9 (5.5 mm), or size required to obtain correct gauge. Crochet hook size G (4.25 mm). Nine bobbins.

GAUGE:
18 sts = 4"; 20 rows = 4".

SPECIAL ABBREVIATION:
Wyif: With yarn in front.

AFGHAN:
Wind 5 A bobbins and 2 each B and C; set aside.

With A, cast on 230 sts. Work in stockinette st (k 1 row, p 1 row) for 12 rows; fasten off. Begin using bobbins and pat st.

Row 1 (right side): * With A, k 10; with B, k 1, (sl 1 wyif, k 1) twenty-two times; with A, k 10; with C, k 1, (sl 1 wyif, k 1) twenty-two times; repeat from * once, k 10 A.

Row 2: * P 10 A, p 45 C, p 10 A, p 45 B, repeat from * once, p 10 A.

Row 3: * With A, k 10, (sl 1 wyif, k 1) twenty-two times, k 1, repeat from * three times, k 10.

Row 4: With A, purl.

Rows 5–64: Work rows 1–4 fifteen times.

Rows 65, 67, 69, 71, 73, and 75: With A, knit.

Rows 66, 68, 70, 72, 74, and 76: With A, purl. * Work rows 1–76, reversing the placement of colors B and C; work rows 1–76, repeat from * once.

TRIM: With right sides facing, crochet hook and A, attach yarn to any corner. * Sc in 10 sts, ch 3, repeat from * around afghan, sl st to first sc. End off.

TULIP PATCH

Fill your room with spring flowers "fresh" from the garden! These lovely tulips are cross-stitched on single-crochet panels. Create a matching pillow, too.

For how-to information, see Afghan Basics at the back of the book.

AFGHAN

SIZE:
50″ × 66″

MATERIALS:
Bulky-weight acrylic/wool blend (such as Pingouin Iceberg): 53 oz. Ecru, 10½ oz. Dark Green, 1¾ oz. each Light Blue, Deep Blue, Light Rose, Dark Rose. Wooden crochet hook size M (9 mm) or size required to obtain correct gauge. Tapestry needle.

GAUGE:
17 sc and 20 rows = 8″ square.

AFGHAN:
PANEL (make 5): With Ecru, ch 18.

Row 1: Sc in 2nd ch from hook, sc in each ch across—17 sc. Ch 1, turn.

Rows 2–20: Sc in each sc across. Ch 1, turn each row.

Row 21: Ch 3 (counts as 1 dc plus 1 ch), * sk next st, dc in next st, ch 1, repeat from * across, end dc in last st. Ch 1, turn.

Row 22: Sc in first dc, * sc in ch-1 sp, sc in next dc, repeat from * across, end sc in last sp, sc in 2nd ch of ch 3. Ch 1, turn. Repeat rows 2–22 five more times, then repeat rows 2–20 (7 sc squares of 20 rows separated by openwork row). Working down side of panel, work sc in each sc row, 2 sc in each dc row to bottom, 3 sc in corner, sc in each ch across lower edge, 3 sc in corner; work sc on 2nd side as for first side to top of panel; end off.

EMBROIDERY: Using double strand of yarn, work cross-stitches on sc squares, following chart. Each square on chart represents one stitch. On two panels for sides of afghan, work design in first square at bottom, using Light Rose and Dark Rose for tulip. Skip 1 square, embroider 3rd square using Light Blue and Deep Blue for tulip. Embroider 5th square as for first square; embroider 7th square as for 3rd square. On one panel for center, beg in first square at bottom, work tulip colors in reverse (start with Light Blue and Deep Blue).

On 2nd panel, beg in 2nd square from bottom, work tulip with Light Blue and Deep Blue. Skip one square, embroider 4th square with Light Rose and Deep Rose. Embroider 6th square as for 2nd square. On 4th panel, work tulip colors in reverse (work 2nd square from bottom with Light Rose and Deep Rose).

TO JOIN PANELS: Hold 2 panels to be joined with right sides tog. From wrong side, join Ecru in first sc on side of panel facing you. Ch 2, sl st in first sc on 2nd panel. Insert hook down in first sc of 2nd panel and up in 2nd sc, work sl st. Insert hook down in 2nd sc and up in 3rd sc, work sl st. * Skip 1 sc on first panel, dc in next sc, work 2 sl sts on 2nd panel (inserting hook in same sc as last sl st and up in next sc twice), repeat from * across, end dc in last sc on first panel. End off. Join all panels in same way.

BORDER: Rnd 1: With Ecru, from right side, work dc, ch 1 pattern all around afghan, working dc, ch 3, dc in each corner st. Join; end off.

  Rnds 2–5: With Dark Green, work 4 rnds sc, working sc in each st, 3 sc in each corner. Join; end off.

  Rnds 6–9: With Ecru, work 4 more rnds sc. Join; end off.

AFGHAN

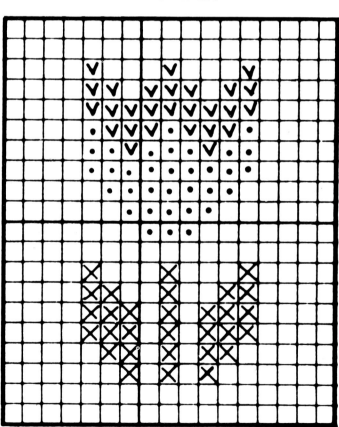

COLOR KEY

⊡ Dark Rose or Deep Blue

Ⓥ Light Rose or Light Blue

☒ Dark Green

PILLOW

SIZE:
15" square

MATERIALS:
Bulky-weight, acrylic-wool blend (such as Pingouin Iceberg): 10½ oz. Ecru; 1¾ oz. each Dark Green, Light Blue, Deep Blue, Light Rose, and Dark Rose. Crochet hook size K (6.5 mm), or size required to obtain correct gauge. Pillow form. Tapestry needle.

GAUGE:
5 sc = 2"; 6 rows = 2".

PILLOW (make 2):
With Ecru, ch 36.

Row 1: Sc in 2nd ch from hook, sc in each ch across—35 sc. Ch 1, turn.

Row 2: Sc in each sc across, ch 1, turn each row. Repeat row 2 until 47 rows have been completed. End off.

EMBROIDERY: Embroider tulips on one piece, following chart. Center one tulip with bottom of stem on row 18. Place a tulip of contrasting color separated by 1 st on both sides of center tulip.

FINISHING:
From right side, with Ecru, sc pieces tog on 3 sides, working sc in each st or row, 3 sc in each corner. Insert pillow form, close last side. With Dark Green, work 2 rows sc around pillow, working 3 sc in each corner. Join; end off.

PILLOW

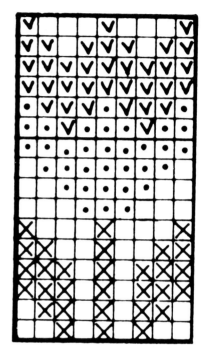

COLOR KEY

- ☐• Dark Rose or Deep Blue
- ☑ Light Rose or Light Blue
- ☒ Dark Green

FROM MY GARDEN

Capture the essence of spring with cheerful bouquets and a watering can overflowing with fresh-cut flowers. The designs are worked in cross-stitch on single crochet.

For how-to information, see Afghan Basics at the back of the book.

SIZE:
52" × 72"

MATERIALS:
Worsted-weight, 4-ply yarn: 42 oz. Off-white; 3 oz. each Lilac and Light Yellow; 10½ oz. each Light Spring Green and Hunter Green; 3½ oz. each Camel, Medium Gold, and Tangerine. Crochet hook size G (4.25 mm), or size required to obtain correct gauge. Tapestry needle.

GAUGE:
4 sc = 1"; 4 rows = 1".

AFGHAN:

CENTER SECTION: With Off-white, ch 87.

Row 1: Sc in 2nd ch from hook and in each ch across—86 sc. Ch 1, turn.

Rows 2–154: Sc in each sc across. Ch 1, turn each row. At end of row 154, end off.

EMBROIDERY: Beginning on row 31 of center section and placing first cross-stitch on 13th st from right-hand edge, following chart 1, embroider design in cross-stitch. With Camel, outline boxes below watering can with outline stitch on lower and right edge of each box.

BORDER SECTIONS (make 14): With Off-white, ch 36.

Row 1: Sc in 2nd ch from hook and in each ch across—35 sc. Ch 1, turn.

Rows 2–41: Sc in each sc across. Ch 1, turn each row. At end of row 41, end off.

EMBROIDERY: Following chart 2, embroider design in cross-stitch on each border section.

EDGING: Rnd 1: With Hunter Green, work 1 row of sc around center section, working sc, ch 1, sc in each corner. Join with sl st in first sc. Ch 1.

Rnd 2: Sc in each sc, sc, ch 1, sc in each sp at corner. Join; end off.

Rnd 3: With Spring Green, work * sc in next sc, dc in next sc on rnd 1, repeat from * around, working sc, ch 1, sc in each corner. Join; end off.

Rnds 4–6: With Hunter Green, work 3 rnds of sc, working sc, ch 1, sc in each corner. Join each rnd. End off.

Work same edging around each border section.

CHART 1 – WATERING CAN

COLOR KEY

⠐ Light Yellow		☑ Tangerine
⊙ Gold		⁼ Lilac
◪ Hunter Green	⫿ Light Green	• Camel

FINISHING:

With Spring Green, sc border sections together and to center section on right side of work to form ridges on right side.

BORDER: Rnd 1: With Spring Green, sc in each sc around afghan, working sc, ch 1, sc in each corner.

   Rnd 2: * Sc in 5 sc, ch 3, sl st in last sc, repeat from * around. Join; end off.

CHART 2 – BORDER

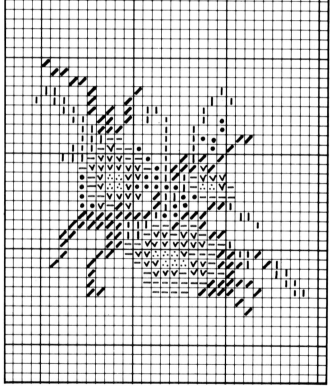

COLOR KEY

⊡ **Light Yellow**
⊙ **Gold**
◪ **Hunter Green**
Ⅱ **Light Green**
Ⅴ **Tangerine**
⊟ **Lilac**

FLOWER DIAMONDS

Rich browns and ecru complement one another in this stylish accent piece. Worked throughout in afghan stitch, panels feature popcorns, bobbles, and embroidered flowers.

For how-to information, see Afghan Basics at the back of the book.

SIZE:
47″ × 60″, plus fringe

MATERIALS:
Worsted-weight, acrylic yarn: 48 oz. Natural; 12 oz. Camel. Persian-type yarn, 12½-yd. skeins: 1 skein Dark Brown; 2 skeins Medium Brown; 2 skeins Camel. Crochet hook size H (5 mm), or size required to obtain correct gauge. Tapestry needle.

GAUGE:
7 sts = 2″; 11 rows = 4″ (afghan st).

BOBBLE:
(Yo hook, draw up a lp in st) three times, yo and through all 7 lps on hook.

POPCORN:
5 dc in sp, drop lp from hook; insert hook in first dc of group, draw dropped lp through, ch 1 tightly.

AFGHAN:
NARROW PANEL (make 4): With Camel and afghan hook, ch 9.

Row 1: Draw up a lp in 2nd ch from hook and in each remaining ch—9 lps on hook.

To Work Lps Off: Yo hook, pull through first lp, * yo hook, pull through next 2 lps, repeat from * across until 1 lp remains. Lp that remains on hook always counts as first st of next row.

Row 2: Keeping all lps on hook, sk first vertical bar, (pull up a lp under next vertical bar) three times, work bobble in next vertical bar (see Bobble), (pull up a lp under next vertical bar) four times—9 lps on hook. Work lps off as before.

Row 3: Keeping all lps on hook, sk first vertical bar, (pull up a lp under next vertical bar) twice, work bobble in next vertical bar, pull up a lp under next vertical bar, work bobble in next vertical bar, (pull up a lp under next vertical bar) three times. Work lps off as before.

Row 4: Repeat row 2.

Row 5: Keeping all lps on hook, sk first vertical bar, pull up a lp under next vertical bar and under each vertical bar across. Work lps off as before.

Row 6: Repeat row 2.
Row 7: Repeat row 5.
Row 8: Repeat row 2.
Row 9: Repeat row 5.
Row 10: Repeat row 2.
Row 11: Repeat row 5.

Repeat rows 2–11, fifteen times (sixteen times in all), then repeat rows 2–5.

Last Row: Sl st in next vertical bar and in each vertical bar across. Drop lp; pick up lp with crochet hook size H.

EDGING: **Row 1:** Ch 2, sc in corner sp, sc in each row down side of panel to lower corner, sc, ch 2, sc in corner, sc in each ch across to next corner, sc, ch 2, sc in corner, sc in each row up side of panel to top corner, sc, ch 2, sc in corner, sc in each sl st across top of panel, sl st in ch-2 sp. End off.

Row 2: Join Natural in ch-2 sp of corner. Ch 3; working down side of panel, popcorn in next sc (see Popcorn), * ch 1, sk next sc, popcorn in next sc, repeat from * across, end ch 1, dc in corner sp. Ch 1, turn.

Row 3 (wrong side): Sc in dc, * sc in ch-1 sp, sc in popcorn, repeat from * across, end sc in top of ch-3. Ch 1, turn.

Row 4 (right side): Sc in each sc across. End off.

Beginning at lower corner on opposite side of panel, work rows 2–4 of edging.

WIDE PANEL (make 3): With Natural and afghan hook, ch 25.

Row 1: Work in afghan st on 25 sts.

Row 2: Pick up 12 lps (lp on hook at beg of row always counts as first lp), bobble in next vertical bar, pick up 12 lps. Work lps off.

Row 3: Pick up 11 lps, bobble in next vertical bar, pick up 1 lp, bobble in next vertical bar, pick up 11 lps. Work lps off.

Row 4: Pick up 10 lps, bobble in next vertical bar, pick up 3 lps, bobble in next vertical bar, pick up 10 lps. Work lps off.

Row 5: Pick up 9 lps, bobble in next vertical bar, pick up 5 lps, bobble in next vertical bar, pick up 9 lps. Work lps off.

Row 6: Pick up 8 lps, bobble, pick up 7 lps, bobble, pick up 8 lps. Work lps off.

Row 7: Pick up 7 lps, bobble, pick up 9 lps, bobble, pick up 7 lps. Work lps off.

Row 8: Pick up 6 lps, bobble, pick up 11 lps, bobble, pick up 6 lps. Work lps off.

Row 9: Pick up 5 lps, bobble, pick up 13 lps, bobble, pick up 5 lps. Work lps off.

Row 10: Pick up 4 lps, bobble, pick up 15 lps, bobble, pick up 4 lps. Work lps off.

Row 11: Pick up 3 lps, bobble, pick up 17 lps, bobble, pick up 3 lps. Work lps off.

Row 12: Repeat row 10.
Row 13: Repeat row 9.
Row 14: Repeat row 8.
Row 15: Repeat row 7.
Row 16: Repeat row 6.
Row 17: Repeat row 5.
Row 18: Repeat row 4.
Row 19: Repeat row 3.
Row 20: Repeat row 2.

Repeat rows 3–20, eight times (nine times in all). Work 1 row even, without bobbles.

Last Row: Sl st in next vertical bar and in each vertical bar across. Drop lp; pick up lp with crochet hook size H.

EDGING: **Row 1:** Work as for edging of narrow panel. Do not end off. With Natural, work rows 2–4 as for edging of narrow panel. Work same edging on other side of panel.

EMBROIDERY: With Dark Brown embroidery yarn in tapestry needle, embroider a ½"-diameter flower center in satin stitch at center of each diamond on wide panels. With Camel or Medium Brown embroidery yarn, embroider 6 petals ¾" long in satin stitch around flower center; on 2 wide panels for outer panels, embroider first flower at bottom with Camel, next with Medium Brown; alternate colors to top. On remaining wide panel for center panel of afghan, embroider first flower at bottom with Medium Brown, next with Camel, alternate colors to top.

FINISHING:

Sew panels tog with Natural, picking up back lps of sc on edges, alternating narrow and wide panels.

FRINGE: Cut Natural and Camel in 12″ lengths. Using 5 strands tog for each fringe, knot a fringe in every 3rd st across top and bottom of afghan, matching colors of panels.

NOSEGAYS FOR SPRING

Pastel posies bearing promises of summer adorn this lovely crocheted afghan. With its delicate joinings and lacy trim, it is just the right covering for early-spring mornings.

For how-to information, see Afghan Basics at the back of the book.

SIZE:
56" × 62"

MATERIALS:
Sport-weight, 3-ply yarn: 35 oz. Natural. DMC Floralia 3-ply Persian wool, 20 skeins #7605 Pink, 8 skeins each #7342 Green and #7689 Pale Pink, 7 skeins each #7811 Lilac and #7921 Blue, 6 skeins #7341 Light Green, 5 skeins #7743 Yellow. Afghan hook size H (5 mm). Crochet hook size G (4.5 mm), or size required to obtain correct gauge. Tapestry needle.

GAUGE:
5 sts = 1" (afghan st).

AFGHAN STITCH:
Ch desired number of sts.

Row 1: Keeping all lps on hook, pull up a lp in 2nd ch from hook and in each ch across.

To Work Lps Off: Yo hook, pull through first lp, * yo hook, pull through next 2 lps, repeat from * across until 1 lp remains.

Row 2: Keeping all lps on hook, sk first vertical bar, pull up a lp under next vertical bar and under each vertical bar across to last st, insert hook under last vertical bar and in loop at back of bar, pull up a lp. Work lps off as before.

AFGHAN:

PANEL (make 5): With afghan hook, ch 32. Work row 1 of afghan stitch—32 lps. Work row 2 of afghan stitch.

Repeat row 2 until there are 170 rows. Sc in each vertical bar across, 3 sc in corner, sc in each row to lower edge, 3 sc in corner, sc in each ch across lower edge, 3 sc in corner, sc in each row to top, 3 sc in corner, join with sl st to first sc. End off.

EMBROIDERY: Using all 3 ply of embroidery wool, following chart, embroider 4 flower designs in cross-stitch on each panel. Begin first design on 7th row of panel, work 29 rows to top of chart. * Skip 14 rows, repeat design. Repeat from *, ending with 6 free rows at top of panel.

INSERTION (make 4): With crochet hook, ch 24.

Row 1: Dc in 8th ch from hook, dc in each of next 13 ch, ch 2, sk 2 ch, dc in last ch. Ch 5, turn.

Row 2: Sk 2 ch, dc in each of next 6 dc, ch 3, sk 2 dc, dc in each of next 6 dc, ch 2, sk 2 ch, dc in 3rd ch of turning ch. Ch 5, turn.

Row 3: Dc in each of next 4 dc, ch 5, dc in ch-3 sp, ch 5, sk 2 dc, dc in each of next 4 dc, ch 2, dc in 3rd ch of turning ch. Ch 5, turn.

Row 4: Dc in each of next 2 dc, ch 5, hdc in next ch-5 sp, ch 3, hdc in next ch-5 sp, ch 5, sk 2 dc, dc in each of last 2 dc, ch 2, dc in 3rd ch of turning ch. Ch 5, turn.

Row 5: Dc in next 2 dc, dc in each of next 2 ch, ch 4, dc in next ch-3 sp, ch 4, sk 3 ch, dc in each of next 2 ch, dc in each of next 2 dc, ch 2, dc in 3d ch of turning ch. Ch 5, turn.

Row 6: Dc in each of next 4 dc, dc in each of next 2 ch, ch 3, sk 2 ch of next ch-4 sp, dc in each of next 2 ch, dc in each of next 4 dc, ch 2, dc in 3rd ch of turning ch. Ch 5, turn.

Row 7: Dc in each of next 6 dc, 2 dc in ch-3 sp, dc in each of next 6 dc, ch 2, dc in 3rd ch of turning ch. Ch 5, turn. Repeat rows 2–7 until there are 19 patterns; end row 7. Do not end off. Ch 1. Working along side edge, work 2 sc in end sp, * sc in next sp, 2 sc in next sp, repeat from * to lower edge. End off. Beg in first sp at bottom edge on other long edge, work to correspond to first edge.

FINISHING:

From wrong side, sew insertions between panels, picking up top loop only of each sc on both edges.
BORDER: From right side, join yarn in corner sc at bottom edge of afghan.

Row 1: Ch 5, sk 2 sc, dc in next sc (ch 2, sk 2 sc, dc in next sc) nine times, ch 2, sk seam, dc in corner ch of insertion, ch 2, dc in ch below first dc of insertion, (ch 2, sk 2 sts, dc in next st) four times, ch 2, * dc in corner ch, ch 2, sk seam and next sc, dc in next sc, (ch 2, sk 2 sc, dc in next sc) ten times, ch 2, sk seam, dc in corner ch of insertion, ch 2, dc in ch below first dc of insertion, ch 2, sk 1 st, dc in next st, (ch 2, sk 2 sts, dc in next st) three times, ch 2, sk 1 st, dc below last dc of insertion, ch 2, sk 2 ch, repeat from * across, end (ch 2, sk 2 sc, dc in next sc) ten times—85 sps. Ch 5, turn.

Row 2: Dc in next dc, * ch 2, dc in next dc, repeat from * across, end ch 2, sk 2 ch of ch 5, dc in next ch—85 sps. Ch 5, turn.

Row 3: Tr in first sp, ch 7; holding back on hook last lp of each tr, work 3 tr in same sp, yo and through all lps on hook (3-tr cluster made), ch 7, work 2-tr cluster in same sp, * sk next sp, dc in next sp, sk next sp; in next sp work 2-tr cluster, ch 7, 3-tr cluster, ch 7 and 2-tr cluster, repeat from * across. End off.

Work same border across top of afghan.

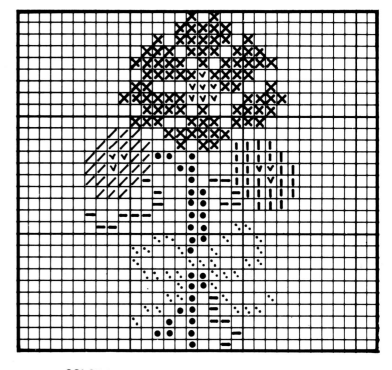

COLOR KEY

☒	Pink	⊟	Lt. Green
⋰	Lt. Pink	▯	Lilac
●	Green	◪	Blue
		☑	Yellow

GERANIUM

Geraniums burst into bloom on this striking black afghan with its matching pillow—two eyecatching additions to any room.

For how-to information, see Afghan Basics at the back of the book.

SIZE:
Afghan, 66″ × 47″; pillow, 14″ square

MATERIALS:
Worsted-weight, 4-ply yarn: 45½ oz. Black; 6½ oz. Red; 3½ oz. Green; small amount Yellow. Crochet hook size J (6 mm), or size required to obtain correct gauge. Tapestry needles. Materials for tracing embroidery designs. White crepe paper. Pillow form, 14″ square.

GAUGE:
15 sc = 4″.

AFGHAN:
SQUARE (make 12): With black, ch 52.

Row 1: Sc in 2nd ch from hook and in each ch across—51 sc. Ch 1, turn.

Row 2: Sc in each sc across. Ch 1, turn each row.

Work even in sc until piece is square. Work 1 rnd sc around square, working 3 sc in each corner.

Note: Make sure each square is the same size.

EDGING: Join Red in corner, ch 3 for first dc, 5 dc in corner st, * sk 3 sc, 3 dc in next st, repeat from * around working 6 dc in each corner. Join; end off.

EMBROIDERY: Draw lines across Motif A pattern, connecting grid lines. Enlarge motif by copying on paper ruled in 1″ squares. Trace motif onto bond paper. Trace motif onto 12″ square of crepe paper. Baste crepe paper pattern on crocheted square. Working through crepe paper, embroider flowers in Red with satin stitch. With Green, embroider stems in outline stitch, outline of leaves in chain stitch; fill in leaves with French knots. With Yellow, work 3 French knots at center of each flower. Tear away paper when embroidery is completed. Work 6 squares with this design.

Motif B is given actual size. Trace motif onto bond paper. Trace 3 motifs as given and 3 in mirror image. Embroider same as Motif A.

FINISHING:
Sew squares tog with Red, picking up back lps on sts only. Place A motifs at the 4 corners and 2 at center. Place B motifs as given at left side and center bottom of afghan. The B motifs in mirror image are for right side and center top of afghan.

PILLOW:
Make 2 Black squares same as afghan. Embroider one square with geranium design. With wrong sides tog, sew squares tog around 3 sides. Edge pillow same as afghan squares, working through both thicknesses on three sewn sides and through front square only on fourth side. Insert pillow form. Sew fourth side closed.

Motif A

1 sq. = 1"

Motif B

Actual-Size Pattern

MIDNIGHT MAGIC

Create this beautiful striped coverlet, conveniently worked in separate panels. An unusual combination of embossing and embroidery dramatically enhances the design.

For how-to information, see Afghan Basics at the back of the book.

SIZE:
57″ × 75½″

MATERIALS:
Worsted-weight, 4-ply yarn: 16 oz. Medium Blue; 24 oz. each White and Navy. Aluminum afghan hook, 14″ long, size I (5.5 mm), or size needed to obtain correct gauge. Crochet hook size G (4.5 mm).

GAUGE:
7 sts = 2″; 13 rows = 4″.

AFGHAN STITCH:
Ch desired number of sts.

Row 1: Insert hook in top lp only of 2nd ch from hook, draw up a lp, * insert hook in top lp of next ch, draw up a lp; repeat from * across.

To Work Lps Off: Yo and draw through 1 lp on hook, * yo and draw through 2 lps on hook; repeat from * across until 1 lp remains on hook. Lp that remains on hook always counts as first st of next row.

Row 2: Keeping all lps on hook, sk first vertical bar, * insert hook under next vertical bar, yo and draw up a lp, repeat from * across. Work off lps as before. Repeat row 2 for afghan stitch.

AFGHAN:
Note: As each panel is completed, mark bottom with safety pins. This will insure all panels being joined in proper manner.

WHITE PANELS (make 3): With White and afghan hook, ch 26. Work in afghan st for 229 rows. Bind off. Following Chart A, embroider in cross-stitch.

BLUE PANELS (make 2): With Medium Blue and afghan hook, ch 26. Work in afghan st for 2 rows.

Row 3: Pick up 26 lps. Work off 5 lps, ch 4 (picot), work off 8 lps, ch 4 (picot), work off 8 lps, ch 4 (picot), work off remaining 5 lps.

Row 4: Pick up 26 lps. Work off 4 lps, picot, work off 2 lps, picot, work off 6 lps, picot, work off 2 lps, picot, work off 6 lps, picot, work off 2 lps, picot, work off remaining 4 lps.

Row 5: Pick up 26 lps. Work off 3 lps, picot, (work off 4 lps, picot) five times, work off remaining 3 lps.

Row 6: Repeat row 4.

Row 7: Pick up 26 lps. Work off 5 lps, picot, (work off 4 lps, picot) four times, work off remaining 5 lps.

Row 8: Pick up 26 lps. Work off 10 lps, picot, work off 6 lps, picot, work off 10 lps.

Row 9: Pick up 26 lps. Work off 7 lps, picot, (work off 4 lps, picot) three times, work off 7 lps. Continue to work picot pattern as established, following Chart 2 for placement of picots.

Row 16: Work in afghan st.

Row 17: Pick up 26 lps. Work off 13 lps, picot, work off 13 lps. Continue to work picot pattern from chart, having one plain row of afghan st between picot patterns; end with 2 plain afghan st rows for a total of 229 rows. Bind off.

EDGING: From right side, with Navy and G hook, work 1 row sc on each long edge of all 5 panels, working 1 sc in each row. Do not crochet across ends of panels.

CHEVRON STRIPS (make 6): With Navy and afghan hook, ch 9. Work even in afghan st for 3 rows.

Row 4: Draw up a lp in each of 3 vertical bars (4 lps on hook), yo hook three times, draw up a lp in 2nd vertical bar of 3rd row below, (yo and through 2 lps) three times (5 lps on hook), yo hook three times, draw up a lp in 8th st of 3rd row below, (yo and through 2 lps) four times, sk center bar of last row, draw up a lp in each of last 4 bars (9 lps on hook), work off lps in same manner as before.

Row 5. Work even in afghan st. Repeat rows 4 and 5 until there is a total of 229 rows. Bind off.

JOINING: With White and G hook, having wrong sides of panels and strips tog, crochet panels and strips tog, working sc in sc of wide panels and in corresponding row on chevron strips. Be sure to start at bottom of pieces and alternate as follows: chevron strip, white panel, chevron strip, blue panel, chevron strip, white panel, chevron strip, blue panel, chevron strip, white panel, chevron strip. From right side, with White, work 1 row sc on long outer edges of first and last chevron strips. Weave in all ends on wrong side.

BORDER: **Rnd 1:** From right side, with Navy and G hook, work 3 sc in any corner st, sc in each st around afghan, 3 sc in each corner. Sl st in first sc. End off. Steam ends of afghan lightly to ensure it will lie flat, being careful not to flatten picot or chevron designs.

Rnd 2: Join White in center st of any corner, ch 3, yo and draw up a lp about ¾" in same st (draw up all lps about ¾"), (yo, draw up a lp in same st) twice, yo and through all 7 lps on hook (cluster made), * ch 2, (yo, draw up a lp in same st) three times, yo and through all 7 lps on hook (cluster made), repeat from * once, ** ch 1, sk 1 sc, cluster in next sc, repeat from ** to next corner, work 3 clusters with ch-2 between clusters in corner sc, repeat from first ** around, end ch 1, sl st in top of first cluster.

Rnd 3: Ch 1, sc in first cluster, 2 sc in next sp, sc in next cluster, 2 sc in next sp, * sc in next cluster, sc in next sp, repeat from * around, working 2 sc in each corner sp; sl st in first sc. End off.

CHART A—White Panel

CHART B—Blue Picot Panel

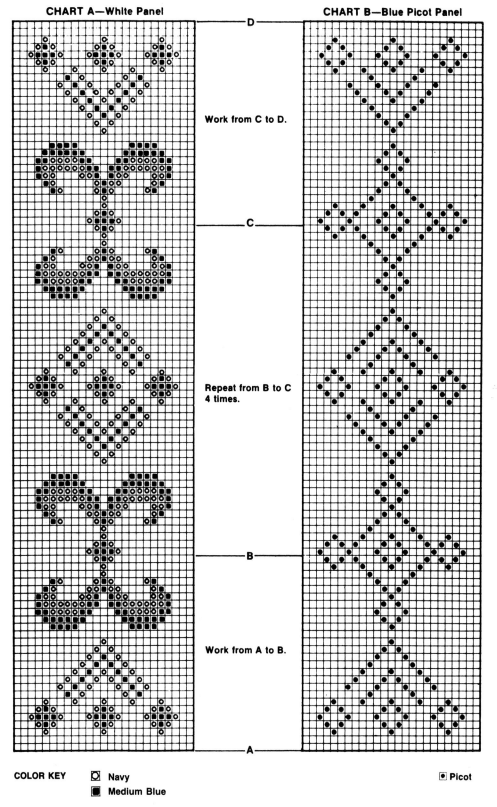

D

Work from C to D.

C

Repeat from B to C
4 times.

B

Work from A to B.

A

COLOR KEY ⬚ Navy

⬛ Medium Blue

⊡ Picot

QUILT CHECK

A favorite with quilters, the "nine-patch" check also adapts beautifully to crochet. Work up several companion pillows.

For how-to information, see Afghan Basics at the back of the book.

SIZE:
Afghan, 48″ × 65″
Square Pillow, 14″ × 14″
Oblong Pillow, 14″ × 20″

MATERIALS:
Worsted-weight, 4-ply yarn: 24½ oz. Bright Violet (A); 17½ oz. Red (B); 10½ oz. Medium Blue (C); 7 oz. Teal (D); 3½ oz. each Black (E), Ecru (F), Gray Heather (G), Green (H), Yellow (I), Dark Violet (J), Purple (K), and Light Rose (L). Crochet hook size D (3.25 mm), or size required to obtain correct gauge. Pillow form, 14″ square. Fiberfill. Fabric, ¼ yd. for each pillow.

GAUGE:
16 sts = 4″; 8 rows = 4″.

AFGHAN:
Note: Afghan can be made with 24 squares joined together or by making 4 strips before adding border.

SQUARE 1: With C, ch 38.
Row 1: Following chart from A to B; with K, dc in 4th ch from hook (counts as 2 dc), dc in next 2 ch; with F, dc in next 4 ch; with K, dc in next 4 ch; with B, dc in

next 12 ch; with E, dc in next 4 ch; with H, dc in next 4 ch; with E, dc in next 4 ch. Ch 2, turn each row.

Row 2: Following chart from B to A; with E, dc in next 4 dc; with H, dc in next 4 dc; with E, dc in next 4 dc; with B, dc in next 12 dc; with K, dc in next 4 dc; with F, dc in next 4 dc; with K, dc in next 4 dc.

Rows 3 and 4: With F, dc in next 4 dc; with K, dc in next 4 dc; with F, dc in next 4 dc, with B, dc in next 12 dc; with H, dc in next 4 dc; with E, dc in next 4 dc; with H, dc in next 4 dc. Work in reverse for row 4, following chart.

Rows 5 and 6: Repeat rows 1 and 2.

Rows 7–12: Follow chart, working first 12 and last 12 dc in B; center 12 dc in check pat, alternating A and D every 4 dc.

Rows 13–18: Follow chart, working first 12 dc in check pat, alternating I and E every 4 dc; center 12 dc in B; last 12 dc in check pat, alternating J and L every 4 dc. With C, work 1 row dc. End off.

Following chart, work 23 more squares, always having B dc's in same place and check pats in different color combinations, omitting B and C. With A, work 1 row dc to cast-on edge of each square.

JOINING: Arrange squares on a large flat surface, making sure the colors are different for each of the adjoining squares with contrasting center check pats. With C, dc along sides, picking up 2 sts for every dc—240 dc. Join the strips tog with darning needle and yarn, making sure to match each stitch carefully so that centers correspond. From wrong side, with C, work 1 rnd dc around entire

afghan, working (dc, ch 1, dc) in each corner. End off.

BORDERS: LONG SIDES: With A, work 1 row dc on long sides, adding 1 st at corner. Ch 2, turn. Continue in dc for 13 rows. End off.

SHORT SIDES: Working across A edge: with D, dc in 28 sts; with A, dc in 164 sts; with D, dc in 28 sts. Continue in dc as established for 13 rows. End off.

EDGING: Row 1: With B, work 1 rnd dc around entire afghan, working (dc, ch 1, dc) in each corner. Ch 2, turn.

Row 2: With B, work 1 rnd sc around entire afghan, working 3 sc in ch-1 at each corner. End off.

SQUARE PILLOW:

Following chart from A to B on odd-numbered rows, from B to A on even-numbered rows, work 1 square for 18 rows.

EDGING: Rnd 1: With C, work 1 rnd dc around square, working (2 dc, ch 1, 2 dc) in each corner.

Rnd 2: With C, work 1 rnd dc around square, working (dc, ch 1, dc) in each corner. End off.

BORDERS: SHORT SIDES: With A, work 6 rows dc on top and bottom of square. End off.

LONG SIDES: Working long sides, with D, dc in 12 sts; with A, dc in 44 sts; with D, dc in 12 dc. Continue in dc as established for 6 rows. With B, work 1 rnd dc around entire pillow working (dc, ch 1, dc) in each corner. With B, work 1 rnd sc around entire pillow, working 3 sc in each corner. End off.

OBLONG PILLOW:

With C, ch 62. Follow chart from A to B once, from C to B once on odd-numbered rows, from B to C once, from B to A once on even-numbered rows for 18 rows. Work edges to correspond to square pillow.

TO MAKE PILLOW: Cut out pillow front from fabric 15″ × 15″ for square pillow, 15″ × 21″ for oblong pillow. Cut pillow back same size. Right sides together, stitch pillow front and back together, making ½″ seams and leaving an opening in one side for turning. Turn pillow to right side. Stuff firmly with fiberfill, or insert pillow form. Turn in raw edges and slip-stitch opening closed.

AFGHAN and PILLOW CHART

J	L	J		B			I	E	I
L	J	L					E	I	E
J	L	J					I	E	I
	B		A	D	A			B	
			D	A	D				
			A	D	A				
E	H	E		B			K	F	K
H	E	H					F	K	F
E	H	E					K	F	K

B   C   A

HARVEST GLOW

Create an afghan you will cherish forever with this unusually elegant design. The rich cross-stitch emboidery is beautifully framed with traditional crocheted "cables."

For how-to information, see Afghan Basics at the back of the book.

SIZE:
56″ × 68″

MATERIALS:
Worsted-weight, 4-ply yarn: 32 oz. Off-white; 18 oz. Dark Peach; 16 oz. Cocoa Brown; 4 oz. Olive; 3 oz. Light Peach or Shaded Oranges. Afghan hook size H (5 mm), or size required to obtain correct gauge. Crochet hook size H (5 mm). Tapestry needle.

GAUGE:
7 sts = 2″; 7 rows = 2″.

AFGHAN STITCH:
Ch desired number of sts.

Row 1: Keeping all lps on afghan hook, pull up a lp in 2nd ch from hook and in each ch across.

To Work Lps Off: Yo hook, pull through first lp, *yo hook, pull through next 2 lps, repeat from * across until 1 lp remains. Lp that remains on hook always counts as first st of next row.

Row 2: Keeping all lps on hook, sk first vertical bar, pull up a lp under next vertical bar and under each vertical bar across. Work lps off as before. Repeat these two rows for afghan stitch.

AFGHAN:

WIDE PANEL (make 3): With Off-white, ch 34. Work in plain afghan st for 223 rows.

When 223 rows have been worked, sl st in each vertical bar across last row. End off.

Embroidery: Embroider panels in cross-stitch, beginning on 3rd row of panel. Repeat chart 1 from bottom to top of chart, rows 3–63 three times; then repeat rows 3–37.

NARROW PANEL (make 2): With Cocoa, ch 13. Work in plain afghan st on 13 sts for 223 rows. Sl st across last row. End off.

Embroidery: Embroider panels in cross-stitch, beginning on first row of panel and repeating rows 1–10 of chart 2 to top; then repeat rows 1–3.

BORDER PANELS: With Dark Peach, ch 224.

Row 1: Sc in 2nd ch from hook and in each ch across—223 sc. Ch 1, turn.

Row 2: Sc in first sc, * ch 4, sk 2 sc, sl st in next sc, turn, sl st in first ch, sc in next 3 ch, turn, sc in 2 skipped sc, repeat from * across, sc in last st. Ch 1, turn.

Row 3: Sc in each sc and under each ch sp across—223 sc.

Make 5 more border panels the same. With Cocoa, make 4 border panels the same.

With Dark Peach, from right side, sc a Dark Peach border panel to each side of each Off-white panel, working sc through each row of wide panel and each sc of border panel.

With Cocoa, from right side, sc a Cocoa border panel to each side of Cocoa panels in same way.

FINISHING:

Sew 5 panels together.

EDGING: With Dark Peach, sc around entire afghan, working 3 sc in each corner.

Rnd 2: * Sc in 4 sc, ch 3, sl st in 3rd ch from hook for picot, repeat from * around, working sc, picot, sc in each corner st. Join, end off.

Chart 1

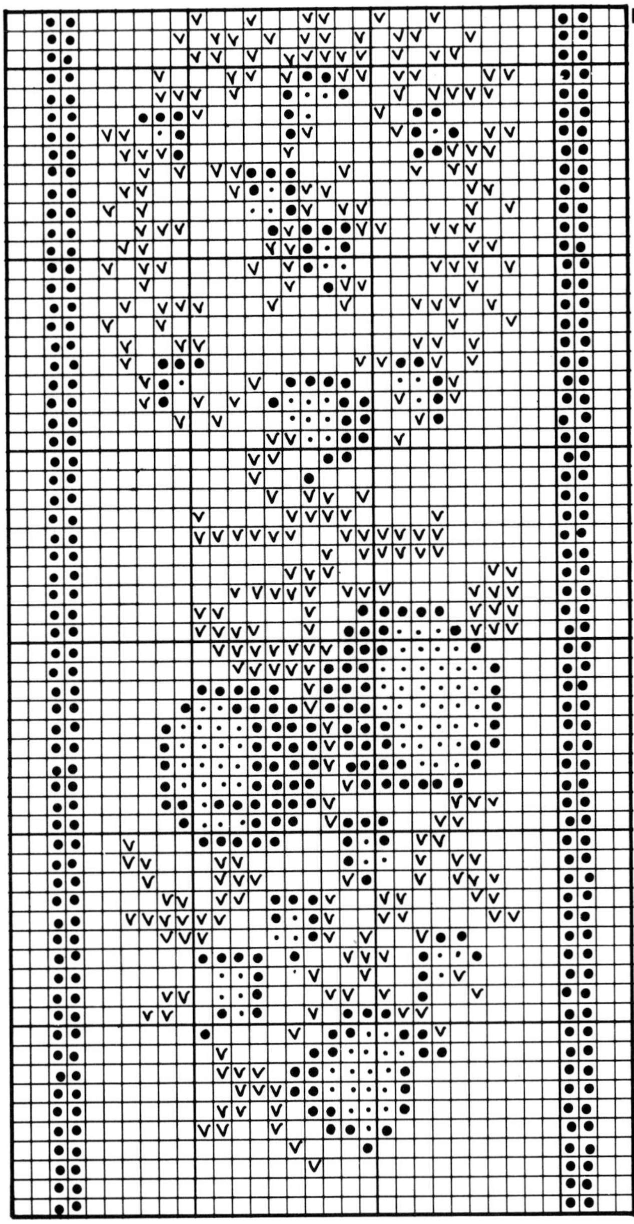

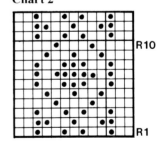

COLOR KEY

● Dark Peach
V Olive
· Light Peach

Chart 2

COLOR KEY

● Off-white
□ Cocoa Brown

LACY AND LUXURIOUS

A selection of light and airy afghans for those times when just a wisp of covering is needed. As cool breezes waft by, curl up under Fanciful Flowers—a carry-along crochet worked in a rainbow of colors. Enjoy the luxury of mohair with the convenience of an all-acrylic yarn in Rose Petals with White Blossoms, or the lovely pastel afghan Peach Fluff. Certain to be favorites are Blue Cables—an easy knit worked in four shades of blue, and Golden Bells—a quick-to-make afghan with a beautiful all-over pattern. And for an easy design that is both feminine and sassy, Cozy Bows is sure to please.

opposite page: *Rose Petals with White Blossoms*

ROSE PETALS WITH WHITE BLOSSOMS

Whisper-soft and light, this beautiful afghan has the charm of an antique coverlet. The lacy flower motifs are linked by simple chain-loop stars.

For how-to information, see Afghan Basics at the back of the book.

SIZE:
52″ × 60″

MATERIALS:
Worsted-weight brushed acrylic yarn (such as Unger's Fluffy): 14 oz. Mauve (A); 5 oz. Off-white (B); 1¾ oz. Green (C). Crochet hook size K (6.5 mm), or size required to obtain correct gauge.

GAUGE:
One motif = 7½″ diameter.

AFGHAN:

FIRST MOTIF: With B, ch 6.

Rnd 1: Dc in 6th ch from hook, (ch 2, dc in same ch) six times, ch 2, sl st in 4th ch of starting ch 6—8 sps.

Rnd 2: Sl st in first sp, sc in same sp, * (ch 5, sl st in 4th ch from hook for picot) twice, ch 1, sc in next sp, repeat from * around, end ch 1, sl st in first sc. End off.

Rnd 3: With A, make lp on hook, sc in ch between 2 picots of any lp, * ch 7, sc in center of next lp between picots, repeat from * around, end ch 7, sl st in first sc.

Rnd 4: In each ch-7 lp work sc, hdc, 9 dc, hdc, sc—8 scallops. Sl st in first sc. End off.

SECOND MOTIF: Work as for first motif through rnd 3.

Rnd 4: In first lp work sc, hdc, 4 dc, sl st in center dc of any scallop of first motif, 5 dc, hdc, sc in same lp of second motif; work sc, hdc, 4 dc in next lp of second motif, sl st in center dc of next scallop of first motif, 5 dc, hdc, sc in same lp of second motif, complete rnd 4 as for first motif.

Make a row of 7 motifs, joining each motif to previous motif as second motif was joined to first motif.

Work a second row of 7 motifs, joining first motif to next 2 scallops of first motif of previous row, then the second motif to next 2 scallops of second motif of previous row and to 2 scallops of first motif of second row. Continue to join motifs in this manner until 8 rows of motifs have been joined.

FILL-IN MOTIF: With C, ch 7, sl st in first ch to form ring. Sc in ring, ch 4, sl st in a joining between 2 motifs, ch 4, (sc in ring, ch 4, sl st in next joining between motifs, ch 4) three times, sl st in first sc. Fill in all spaces between motifs in this manner.

FINISHING:
Run in all yarn ends. Do not block.

PEACH FLUFF

Two textured patterns are combined in this lovely, fluffy crochet. Small diamond shapes are used to fill in the spaces between large motifs.

For how-to information, see Afghan Basics at the back of the book.

SIZE:
53″ × 76″

MATERIALS:
Worsted-weight brushed acrylic yarn (such as Unger's Fluffy): 33¼ oz. Crochet hook size I, or size required to obtain correct gauge.

GAUGE:
Large motif = 10″ from point to opposite point. Medium motif = 6″ from point to opposite point.

AFGHAN:

LARGE MOTIF: First Motif:
Rnd 1: Ch 4, join with sl st in first ch to form ring. Ch 3, 15 dc in ring, sl st in top of ch-3—16 dc (ch 3 counts as 1 dc).

Rnd 2: Ch 3 (counts as hdc and ch 1), * hdc in next dc, ch 1, repeat from * around, sl st in 2nd ch of ch-3.

Rnd 3: Ch 3, 3 dc in same place as sl st, drop lp from hook; insert hook in top of ch-3, draw dropped lp through (popcorn made), 2 dc in ch-1 sp, dc around post of hdc (insert hook down to the right of st, up to the left of st), 2 dc in ch-1 sp, * 4 dc in next hdc, drop lp from hook; insert hook in first dc of 4-dc group, draw lp through, 2 dc in ch-1 sp, dc around post of hdc,

2 dc in ch-1 sp, repeat from * around. Sl st in first dc after popcorn.

Rnd 4: Ch 3, dc in next dc, dc around post of next dc, dc in each of next 2 dc, * ch 2, dc in each of next 2 dc, dc around post of next dc (post dc made), dc in each of next 2 dc, repeat from * around, end hdc in 3rd ch of ch-3 (counts as ch-2 sp).

Rnd 5: Ch 3, 2 dc in sp, sk 2 dc, post dc around post dc, * 3 dc, ch 3, 3 dc in next ch-2 sp, post dc around post dc, repeat from *, end 3 dc in first sp, ch 1, dc in 3rd ch of ch-3 (counts as ch-3 sp).

Rnd 6: Ch 3, 2 dc in sp, ch 1, post dc around post dc, ch 1, * 3 dc, ch 3, 3 dc in next ch-3 sp, ch 1, post dc around post dc, ch 1, repeat from *, end 3 dc in first sp, ch 1, dc in top of ch-3.

Rnd 7: Ch 3, 3 dc in sp just formed, ch 1, post dc around post dc, ch 1, * 4 dc, ch 3, 4 dc in next ch-3 sp, ch 1, post dc around post dc, ch 1, repeat from *, end 4 dc in first sp, ch 3, sl st in top of ch-3. End off.

2nd Motif: Work as for first motif through rnd 6.

Rnd 7: Ch 3, 3 dc in sp just formed, ch 1, post dc around post dc, ch 1, 4 dc in next ch-3 sp, ch 1, sc in any ch-3 sp of first motif, ch 1, 4 dc in same sp of 2nd motif, ch 1, post dc around next post dc, ch 1, 4 dc in next ch-3 sp, ch 1, sc in

next ch-3 sp of first motif, ch 1, 4 dc in same sp of 2nd motif (2 points of 2nd motif joined to 2 points of first motif), ch 1, finish rnd as for first motif.

3rd, 4th, and 5th Motifs:

Work as for 2nd motif, joining to 2 points opposite previous joinings. (**Note:** There are 2 free points on each side of each joined motif.)

6th Motif (2nd row of motifs):

Work as for 2nd motif, joining points to 2 free points on side of first motif.

7th, 8th, 9th, and 10th Motifs:

Work as for 2nd motif, joining 2 points to 2 points of previous motif and next 2 points to free points on side of motifs of first row.

Work 5 more rows of 5 motifs, joining motifs in rnd 7 as before, until there are 7 rows of 5 motifs.

MEDIUM MOTIF: Rnd 1: Ch 4, join with sl st in first ch to form ring. Ch 3, 3 dc in ring; drop lp from hook, insert hook in top of ch-3, draw dropped lp through (popcorn), ch 2, dc in ring, ch 2, * 4-dc popcorn in ring, ch 2, dc in ring, ch 2, repeat from * twice, sl st in top of ch-3.

Rnd 2: Ch 3, 3 dc in same place as sl st, form popcorn, ch 1, 2 dc in ch-2 sp, ch 1, post dc around next dc, ch 1, 2 dc in next sp, ch 1, * 4-dc popcorn in next popcorn, ch 1, 2 dc in next sp, ch 1, post dc around next dc, ch 1, 2 dc in next sp, ch 1, repeat from * twice, ch 1, sl st in top of ch-3.

Rnd 3: Ch 3, 3 dc in same place as sl st, form popcorn, ch 1, dc in ch-1 sp, dc in each of 2 dc, ch 1, post dc around post dc, ch 1, dc in each of 2 dc, dc in ch-1 sp, ch 1, * popcorn in popcorn, ch 1, dc in ch-1 sp and in each of 2 dc, ch 1, post dc around post dc, ch 1,

dc in each of 2 dc, dc in ch-1 sp, ch 1, repeat from * twice, sl st in top of ch-3.

Rnd 4 (joining rnd): These medium motifs are joined to the large motifs in the 24 spaces between 4 large motifs. Ch 3, 3 dc in same place as sl st, form popcorn, sc over joining of 2 large motifs, ch 1, dc in ch-1 sp and in each of 3 dc, ch 1, post dc around post dc, sc around post dc of large motif, ch 1, dc in each of 3 dc and in ch-1 sp, ch 1, * work popcorn, sc over joining of large motifs, ch 1, dc in ch-1 sp and in each of 3 dc, ch 1, post dc around post dc, sc around post dc of large motif, ch 1, dc in each of 3 dc and in ch-1 sp, ch 1, repeat from * twice, sl st in top of ch-3. End off.

HALF-MEDIUM MOTIF: Row 1: Ch 4, join with sl st in first ch to form ring. Ch 3; repeat from * of rnd 1 of medium motif until there are 3 popcorns, dc in ring. End off.

Row 2: Join yarn to top of ch-3 at beg of row 1. Ch 3; repeat from * of rnd 2 of medium motif, end popcorn in popcorn, dc in dc. End off.

Row 3: Join yarn to top of ch-3 at beg of row 2. Ch 3; repeat from * of rnd 3 of medium motif, end popcorn in popcorn, dc in dc. End off.

Row 4 (joining row): These half motifs are joined to 2 joined large motifs in the 20 spaces around edge of afghan. Join yarn to top of ch-3 at beg of row 3. Ch 3, sc in ch-3 sp of large motif, popcorn in popcorn, ch 1, dc in ch-1 sp and in each of 3 dc, ch 1, post dc around post dc, sc around post dc of large motif, ch 1, dc in each of 3 dc and in ch-1 sp, repeat from * of rnd 4 of medium motif once, end popcorn in popcorn, sc in ch-3 sp of large motif, dc in dc. End off.

SMALL MOTIF: These small motifs are joined to large motifs in the 58 spaces between each 2 large joined motifs. Ch 6, join with sl st in first ch to form ring. Ch 3, 3 dc in ring, ch 1, sc around post dc of large motif, ch 1, 4 dc in ring, ch 1, sc around joining of medium motif, ch 1, 4 dc in ring, ch 1, sc around post dc of large motif, ch 1, 4 dc in ring, ch 1, sc around joining of medium motif, ch 1, sl st in top of ch-3. End off.

BORDER: Join yarn at beg of any half motif. * Work 2 dc over each dc to center of half motif, dc in center ring, 2 dc over each ch-3 along edge, dc in joining, 2 dc in ch-3 sp of large motif, dc in each of next 4 dc; holding back on hook last lp of each dc, dc in each of next two ch-1 sps, yo and through 3 lps on hook; dc in each of next 4 dc, 2 dc in ch-3 sp, dc in joining, repeat from * around, working 3 dc in each ch-3 sp of large motifs at corners of afghan.

FANCIFUL FLOWERS

Curl up under a blanket of flowers! This luscious afghan, crocheted in fantasy colors, has raised flower motifs for added dimension.

For how-to information, see Afghan Basics at the back of the book.

SIZE:
58″ × 80″

MATERIALS:
Worsted-weight 4-ply yarn: 10½ oz. each Rose (R), Dark Blue (D), Green; 7 oz. White (W); 3½ oz. each Gold (G), Lavender (L), Pink (P), Light Blue (B). Crochet hook size H (5 mm). or size required to obtain correct gauge.

GAUGE:
Each motif is 8″ in diameter.

AFGHAN:
Note: Make first motif. After first motif, each motif will be joined on the last rnd. Work 2 rnds with each color called for.

LARGE ROSE CIRCLE (center of afghan):

MOTIF 1: Rnd 1: With W, ch 5, join with sl st to form ring, ch 1 (counts as first sc), ch 7, (sc in ring, ch 7) five times, sl st in first sc—6 ch-sps.

Rnd 2: (Sl st in each of 7 chs, ch 1, skip sc) six times, sl st in first sl st. Fasten off W.

Rnd 3: Attach G in any ch-1 sp, ch 1 (counts as first sc), ch 3 (hold in back of ch-7 lp, sc in next ch-1 sp, ch 3) five times, sl st in first sc.

Rnd 4: (In ch-3 sp, work 1 sc, 1 hdc, 1 dc, ch 1, 1 dc, 1 hdc, 1 sc, ch 5) six times, sl st in first sc. Fasten off G.

Rnd 5: Join P in any ch-5 lp. Ch 1 (counts as first sc), ch 4, sc in ch-1 sp between 2 dc, ch 4, (sc in ch-5 lp, ch 4, sc in ch-1 sp, ch 4) five times, join with sl st to first sc.

Rnd 6: (In next ch-4 lp, work 1 sc, 1 hdc, 2 dc, ch 1, then in next ch-4 lp work 2 dc, 1 hdc, 1 sc, ch 1) six times. Join with sl st to first sc. Fasten off P.

Rnd 7: Join R in ch-1 between dc's, ch 1 (counts as first sc), (ch 3, in next ch-1 sp work dc, ch 5, dc, ch 3, sc in next ch-1 sp) six times, ending last repeat, ch 1, dc in first sc (counts as last ch 3).

Rnd 8: (Ch 5, sc in next ch-3 lp; in ch-5 lp work 4 dc, ch 1, 4 dc; then sc in next ch-3 lp) six times, sl st in base of first ch-5. Fasten off R.

MOTIF 2: Work as for Motif 1 in the following color sequence:
Rnds 1 and 2: G.
Rnds 3 and 4: P.
Rnds 5 and 6: W.
Rnds 7 and 8: R. Join Motif 2 to Motif 1 as follows on rnd 8: Ch 5, sc in ch-3 lp of Motif 2, work 4 dc in ch-5 lp of Motif 2; holding motifs back to back sc in ch-1 sp between 4 dc of Motif 1 (called joining 1); 4 dc back in same ch-5 lp of Motif 2, sc in next ch-3 of Motif 2; ch 2, sc in ch-5 lp of Motif 1; ch 2, sc in next ch-3 sp of Motif 2 (called joining 2); 4 dc in ch-5 of Motif 2; sc in ch-1 sp between 4 dc of Motif 1; 4 dc back in same ch-5 lp of Motif 2, complete as for rnd 8 of Motif 1.

MOTIF 3: Work as for Motif 1 in the following color sequence:

Rnds 1 and 2: P.
Rnds 3 and 4: W.
Rnds 5 and 6: G.
Rnds 7 and 8: R. On rnd 8, join to Motif 2 in the same manner as Motif 2 was joined to Motif 1. For next 3 motifs, repeat Motifs 1, 2, and 3, joining on rnd 8 to previous motif and on last motif, join one side to previous motif and other side to Motif 1, forming a circle.

CENTER MOTIF: Work as for Motif 1 in the following color sequence:

Rnds 1 and 2: R.
Rnds 3 and 4: P.
Rnds 5 and 6: G.
Rnds 7 and 8: W, joining as follows: Sc over each joining 1 and working joining 2 as was done previously. Center motif is joined to all 6 motifs. See diagram.

LARGE BLUE CIRCLE:

MOTIF 1: Work as Motif 1 of Rose Circle in the following color sequence:

Rnds 1 and 2: W.
Rnds 3 and 4: L.
Rnds 5 and 6: B.
Rnds 7 and 8: D, joining to 1 motif of Rose Circle (see diagram).
Note: All motifs of the Blue Circle are joined tog as for Circle 1, but **at the same time,** you are joining 2 petals to Rose Circle.

MOTIF 2: Rnds 1 and 2: L.
Rnds 3 and 4: B.
Rnds 5 and 6: W.
Rnds 7 and 8: D, joining as explained above on rnd 8.

MOTIF 3: Rnds 1 and 2: B.
Rnds 3 and 4: W.
Rnds 5 and 6: L.
Rnds 7 and 8: D, joining as explained above. Repeat Motifs 1, 2, and 3, making a circle.

CENTER MOTIF: Work as for Motif 1, in following color sequence:

Rnds 1 and 2: D.
Rnds 3 and 4: B.
Rnds 5 and 6: L.
Rnds 7 and 8: W, joining center motif to all six motifs as on Rose Circle.

DIAMOND FILL-IN: In each diamond-shaped sp, work as follows: Using Green, ch 7, join with sl st to form ring. Ch 7 (counts as a dc and ch 5), * sc over joining 1; in ch-sp work 1 sc, 2 hdc, 2 dc; work 2 dc in ring; work a regular joining 2; 2 dc in ring, ch 5; repeat from * four times, end last repeat dc in ring, sl st in 3rd ch of ch-7. Fasten off.

TRIANGLE FILL-IN: In each triangular space, work as follows. Using Green, ch 5, join with sl st to form ring. Work same as Diamond Fill-in, repeat from * three times, end same as for Diamond Fill-in.

EDGE MOTIFS: Work Diamond and Triangle Fill-ins, omitting last joining 2 and working ch 3 instead.

EDGING: With Green, join in any ch-3 sp, * ch 9, sc in ch-1 sp, ch 9, sc in ch-5 sp, ch 9, sc in ch-1 sp, ch 9, sc in ch-3 sp; repeat from * around entire afghan. Join with sl st.

Rnd 2: * In ch-9 sp, work 1 sc, 3 hdc, 4 dc, 3 hdc, 1 sc; repeat from * around. Join with sl st.

BLUE CABLES

Cable twists and garter stitch create the beautiful texture in this knitted afghan of sea- and sky-blue stripes.

For how-to information, see Afghan Basics at the back of the book.

SIZE:
48″ × 60″

MATERIALS:
Worsted-weight, 4-ply yarn: 8 oz. each of 4 blues; A, B, C, and D. Knitting needles No. 11, or size needed to obtain correct gauge. Cable-stitch needle.

GAUGE:
Each strip should measure 6″ in width.

PATTERN STITCH:
Row 1: K 4, p 1, k 3, p 1, k 6, p 1, k 3, p 1, k 4.

Row 2: K 5, p 3, k 1, p 6, k 1, p 3, k 5.

Row 3: K 4, p 1, yo, sl 1, k 2 tog, psso, yo, p 1, sl next 3 sts onto cable needle and hold in front of work, k next 3 sts, k 3 sts from cable needle (cable twist), p 1, yo, sl 1, k 2 tog, psso, yo, p 1, k 4.

Row 4: Repeat row 2.

Row 5: Repeat row 1.

Row 6: Repeat row 2.

Row 7: K 4, p 1, yo, sl 1, k 2 tog, psso, yo, p 1, k 6, p 1, yo, sl 1, k 2 tog, psso, yo, p 1, k 4.

Row 8: Repeat row 2. Repeat these 8 rows for pattern.

AFGHAN:
STRIP (make 2 of each of 4 colors): Cast on 24 sts. K 6 rows (3 ridges) in garter st. Work even in pattern st until there are 38 cable twists, end row 4. K 6 rows (3 ridges) in garter st. Bind off loosely.

FINISHING:
Sew strips tog as follows: A, B, C, D (center of afghan), A, B, C, D. Steam lightly.

GOLDEN BELLS

Cascading bells cover this richly patterned afghan. Knit it in one piece using two separate strands of yarn worked together to achieve the added texture.

For how-to information, see Afghan Basics at the back of the book.

SIZE:
45″ × 52″, plus fringe

MATERIALS:
Worsted-weight, 4-ply yarn: 40 oz. Medium Gold. Knitting needles No. 13, or size required to obtain correct gauge. Crochet hook size J.

GAUGE:
3 sts = 1″; 12 rows = 3¾″ (pat st, double strand of yarn).

PATTERN STITCH:
Pattern is a multiple of 6 sts plus 2.

Row 1 (right side): P 2, * k 4, p 2, repeat from * across.

Row 2: K 2, * p 4, k 2, repeat from * across.

Row 3: Repeat row 1.

Row 4: Repeat row 2.

Row 5: P 2, * k 4; bring yarn to front, sl 4 sts from right-hand needle to left-hand needle; bring yarn to back crossing in front of the 4 k sts, sl same 4 sts from left-hand needle to right-hand needle; pulling yarn tight, p 2, repeat from * across.

Row 6: P 3, * k 2, p 4, repeat from * across, end last repeat p 3.

Row 7: K 3, * p 2, k 4, repeat from * across, end last repeat K 3.

Row 8: Repeat row 6.

Row 9: Repeat row 7.

Row 10: Repeat row 6.

Row 11: K 3, p 2, * k 4; bring yarn to front, sl 4 sts from right-hand needle to left-hand needle; bring yarn to back crossing in front of the 4 k sts, sl same 4 sts from left-hand needle to right-hand needle; pull yarn tight, p 2, repeat from * across.

Row 12: Repeat row 2.

Repeat rows 1–12 for pat.

AFGHAN:
With double strand of yarn, cast on 128 sts loosely. Work even in pat until piece is 52″ long, or desired length. Bind off in ribbing.

FINISHING:
With double strand, work 1 rnd sc loosely around afghan, working sc in every other row and st, 3 sc in each corner. Sl st in first sc. End off.

FRINGE: Cut strands 12″ long. Using 10 strands tog for each fringe, knot a fringe in every 3rd sc on top and bottom edges.

COZY BOW COVERLET

This charming coverlet with wide pink sashing looks light and inviting. The bows are made separately and sewn on. Sweet picot trim finishes the feminine look.

For how-to information, see Afghan Basics at the back of the book.

SIZE:
42" × 58"

MATERIALS:
Sport-weight yarn: 14 oz. Pink (A), 30 oz. Pink-and-white Tweed (B). Crochet hooks sizes F (3.75 mm) and H (5 mm), or size required to obtain correct gauge. Tapestry needle.

GAUGE:
Each motif = 8" square.

SQUARES (make 30): With larger hook and B, ch 2.
Rnd 1: 8 sc in first ch. Do not join, mark beg of rnd.
Rnd 2: * Working in back lp of sts, 3 sc in next sc for corner, sc in next sc, repeat from * around.
Rnds 3–13: Working in back lp, sc in each sc, working 3 sc in each corner.
Rnd 14: Sc in each sc working 3 sc in each corner. End off.

BOWS (make 10): With smaller hook and A, ch 11, turn.
Row 1: Sc in 2nd ch from hook and in each ch across—10 sc. Ch 1, turn each row.
Row 2: Sc in each sc across. Repeat row 2 until piece measures 8" from beg. End off.

STREAMERS (make 20): With smaller hook and A, ch 7.
Row 1: Sc in 2nd ch from hook and in each ch across—6 sc. Ch 1, turn each row.
Row 2: Sc in each sc across. Repeat row 2 until piece measures 4" from beg.
Next Row: Dec 1 sc, sc to end of row.
Next Row: Sc to last 2 sc, dec 1 sc. Repeat last 2 rows until 1 sc remains. End off.

CENTER OF BOW (make 10): With smaller hook and A, ch 7.
Row 1: Sc in 2nd ch from hook and in each ch across—6 sc. Ch 1, turn each row.
Row 2: Sc in each sc across, turn. Repeat row 2 until piece measures 1" from beg. End off.

ASSEMBLE BOW: Sew bow ends tog. Placing seam in center gather along seam pulling tightly, wrap yarn around twice and fasten. Wrap center around bow, sew seam in back. Sew 2 streamers to back of each bow with shaped ends toward the inside.

TO ASSEMBLE SQUARES: With smaller hook and A, connecting squares vertically, ch 7, sl st in first st on first right-hand square,

turn, sc in 2nd ch from hook and in each ch—6 sc. Sl st in corresponding st on second left-hand square, turn, sc in each of 6 sc. Sl st in next st in right-hand square, turn, sc in each of 6 sc. Sl st in corresponding st on left-hand square, turn, sc in back of 6 sc. Continue to join squares in this manner until there are 6 squares in a strip. Make 5 strips. Then join 5 strips with A in the same manner.

BORDER: With right side facing, smaller hook and A, beg in corner of afghan, work * (dc, ch 3, sl st in first ch, dc) all in same st, sk next st, repeat from * around entire afghan.

FINISHING:
Sew on bows alternating one in every other square where center corner connects, having 2 on each strip. Tack points of streamers to afghan.

FLORAL CABLE

Cable and eyelet panels alternate with stockinette stitch in this lacy coverlet. The lavish fern border is knitted separately. Embroidered yellow, pink, and blue flowers add color and charm.

For how-to information, see Afghan Basics at the back of the book.

SIZE:
43½″ × 60½″

MATERIALS:
Worsted-weight, 4-ply yarn: 44 oz. Off-white (MC); tapestry wool, two 8-meter skeins each Rose (A), Blue (C), and Gold (D); 5 skeins Green (B). Circular knitting needles 29″ long, No. 7 (4.5 mm), or size required to obtain correct gauge. Double-pointed needle. Tapestry needle.

GAUGE:
20 sts = 4″; 26 rows = 4″ (stockinette st).

SPECIAL ABBREVIATIONS:
MB: Make bobble: (K 1, p 1, k 1) in next st, turn, p 3, turn, sl as if to k, k 2 tog, psso—bobble made.

CF6: Front cable on 6 stitches: Sl next 3 sts to dp needle and hold in front of work, k 3, k 3 from dp needle.

CB6: Back cable on 6 stitches: Sl next 3 sts to dp needle and hold in back of work, k 3, k 3 from dp needle.

Ssk: Sl next 2 sts knitwise to right-hand needle, insert left-hand needle into front of these 2 sts and k them tog.

PATTERN STITCHES:

LACE PAT A (worked on 11 sts):
Row 1 (right side): K 3, k 2 tog, yo, k 1, yo, ssk, k 3.
Row 2 and All Even Rows: Purl.
Row 3: K 2, k 2 tog, yo, k 3, yo ssk, k 2.
Row 5: K 1, k 2 tog, yo, k 2 MB, k 2, yo, ssk, k 1.
Row 7: K 2, yo, ssk, k 3, k 2 tog, yo, k 2.
Row 9: K 3, yo, ssk, k 1, k 2 tog, yo, k 3.
Row 11: K 4, yo, sl 1 as if to k, k 2 tog, psso, yo, k 4.
Row 12: Purl. Repeat rows 1–12 for lace pat A.

CABLE PAT B (worked on 10 sts):
Rows 1, 3, 7, 9, 13, 15, and 17 (right side): P 2, k 6, p 2.
Row 2 and All Even Rows: K 2, p 6, k 2.
Rows 5 and 11: P 2, CB6, p 2.
Row 18: Repeat row 2. Repeat rows 1–18 for cable pat B.

CABLE PAT C (worked on 10 sts):
Rows 1, 3, 7, 9, 13, 15, and 17 (right side): P 2, k 6, p 2.
Row 2 and All Even Rows: K 2, p 6, k 2.
Rows 5 and 11: P 2, CF6, p 2.
Row 18: Repeat row 2. Repeat rows 1–18 for cable pat C.

AFGHAN:

With MC, cast on 257 sts. Do not join; work back and forth on circular needle.

Row 1 (right side): Working row 1 on all pats, (pat A on 11 sts, pat B on 10 sts, k 10, pat C on 10 sts) six times, pat A on 11 sts.

Row 2: Working row 2 on all pats, (pat A on 11 sts, pat C on 10 sts, p 10, pat B on 10 sts) six times, pat A on 11 sts. Continue in above established pats until afghan measures about 55″ from beg, end pat A row 10. Bind off in pat.

EDGING: With MC, cast on 8 sts.

Row 1 (right side): K 2, (yo, ssk) twice, yo, k 2—9 sts.

Rows 2, 4, 6, 8, and 10: K 2, p to last 2 sts, k 2.

Row 3: K 3, (yo, ssk) twice, yo, k 2—10 sts.

Row 5: K 4, (yo, ssk) twice, yo, k 2—11 sts.

Row 7: K 5, (yo, ssk) twice, yo, k 2—12 sts.

Row 9: K 6, (yo, ssk) twice, yo, k 2—13 sts.

Row 11: K 7, (yo, ssk) twice, yo, k 2—14 sts.

Row 12: Bind off 6 sts, p to last 2 sts, k 2—8 sts. Repeat rows 1–12 until edging when slightly stretched fits around afghan, gathering at corners, end pat row 12. Bind off loosely. Sew on edging joining ends tog.

FINISHING:

Embroider 10 flowers evenly spaced on each stockinette st section, alternating rows of C, A, and D flowers as follows: using lazy daisy stitch, embroider three-petal flowers in C, A, or D and 2-petal leaves in B, with 3 stem stitches in B for stem.

COUNTRY CASUAL

Wherever the mood is relaxed and welcoming, this group of afghans will be right at home. Wrap yourself in a bonnie Brick-Washed Argyle that is easy to crochet, or work up an all-time favorite, Quick-Crochet Granny. For a perfect spring-into-summer project, choose Flower Baskets, knitted in a cotton-type yarn that is an ideal weight for cool summer evenings. There is nothing more versatile than a stripe motif, and we offer two: for crocheters, there is Colorglow with alternating strips of variegated yarn and off-white; and for knitters, Corner To Corner—an easy pattern actually worked from one corner to the other using basic garter stitch. In the Americana tradition, enjoy a charming Folk-Art Tree crocheted in afghan stitch with cross-stitch embroidery. And for an afghan that can be used anywhere you like to "settle in," try a classic fisherman knit, Cozy Aran.

opposite page: *Flower Baskets*

FLOWER BASKETS

This elegant knit will show off the color and texture of fine, cotton-type yarn. Work one square at a time, using a chart for the baskets. Then embroider the delicate flowers.

For how-to information, see Afghan Basics at the back of the book.

SIZE:
40″ × 56″

MATERIALS:
Sport-weight cotton blend or cottonlike yarn (such as Conshohocken's Softball Cotton and Linen): one 2-lb. cone Medium Blue, main color (MC); 14 oz. Natural; 3½ oz. each Rose, Lavender, Green, and Gold. Knitting needles No. 4 (3.5 mm), or size required to obtain correct gauge. Crochet hook size E (3.5 mm). Bobbins. Pale Rose sewing thread.

GAUGE:
5 sts = 1″; 6 rows = 1″

AFGHAN:

BASKET SQUARE (make 18): With MC, cast on 40 sts. Work in stockinette st (k 1 row, p 1 row), following Chart 1. Use separate bobbins of Natural for borders on each side of square. When top of square is reached (48 rows), bind off. Make 17 squares omitting basket design.

EMBROIDERY: Cut 18 strands of Lavender, 8″ long. Draw ends of one strand to front of basket square at sides of basket, as shown on diagram. Tie ends into a bow at center. Tack bow lightly in place with sewing thread. With Green, embroider stems in outline stitch, taking long stitches. With double strand of Lavender, embroider flowers in French knots (circles) and straight stitches. With single strand of Gold embroider straight stitches inside Lavender stitches. Embroider single flower at each of plain squares.

EDGING: Join Natural with crochet hook in lower right-hand corner of a square, 1 row up from bottom edge and 1 st in from side edge. Working loosely, make 3 sc in corner; working up side of square 1 st in from edge, * sk 1 row, sc in next row, repeat from * to top, 3 sc in corner; working across top edge, 1 row below edge, work in sc across, skipping 1 st between sc's. Work remaining corners and edges to correspond, having same number of sc on side edges and same number on top and bottom edges.

FINISHING:
Arrange squares in 7 rows of 5 squares each, alternating basket squares with single flower squares, having a basket square at each corner of afghan. With Natural, weave squares tog on wrong side, picking up nearest loops of sc sts only.

74

Chart 1

☐ Medium Blue
⊡ Natural
⊟ Rose

Embroidery Chart

BRICK-WASHED ARGYLE

An easy argyle adapted for crochet, made of diagonal strips sewn together and plaided with lines of slip stitch.

For how-to information, see Afghan Basics at the back of the book.

SIZE:
54" × 68"

MATERIALS:
Worsted-weight, 4-ply yarn: 35 oz. Light Terracotta (A); 17½ oz. Melon (B); 14 oz. Off-white (C); 10½ oz. Gold (D). Crochet hook size J (6 mm), or size required to obtain correct gauge.

GAUGE:
7 sc = 2"; 11 rows = 3".

AFGHAN:
Afghan is made in 16 strips that run diagonally across the afghan. All increases and decreases are made on outside edges.

FIRST STRIP (lower right-hand corner): With A, ch 2.

Row 1: Sc in 2nd ch from hook. Ch 1, turn each row.

Row 2: 2 sc in sc.

Row 3 (right side): 2 sc in first sc, sc in last sc.

Row 4: Sc in 2 sc, 2 sc in last sc.

Row 5: 2 sc in first sc, sc in each sc across.

Row 6: Sc in each sc to last sc, 2 sc in last sc.

Rows 7–20: Repeat rows 5 and 6 alternately—20 sc.

Row 21: Pull up a lp in each of first 2 sc, yo and through 3 lps on hook (dec made), sc in each sc across.

Row 22: Sc in each sc across to last 2 sc, dec 1 sc over last 2 sc.

Rows 23–38: Repeat rows 21 and 22 alternately—2 sc.

Row 39: Pull up a lp in each sc, yo and through 3 lps on hook—1 sc. End off.

SECOND STRIP: Work as for first strip through row 20. Work even on 20 sc for 36 rows. Work as for first strip rows 21 to end.

THIRD STRIP: Work as for first strip through row 20. Work even on 20 sc for 18 rows. Change to C. When changing colors, work last st of row until there are 2 lps on hook, finish sc with new color. Ch 1, turn. With C, work 18 rows, change to B. With B, work 18 rows, change to A. With A, work 18 rows, then dec at side edge as for first and second strips, working rows 21 to end.

Work strips 4–16, following chart for colors. Each color square on chart is 18 rows long, 20 sts wide. When working strips 8–16, inc in last st of right-side rows, inc in first st of wrong-side rows on first 20 rows. When working strips 10–16, dec at end of right-side rows, dec at beg of wrong-side rows when working top edge of strip.

FINISHING:

Sew strips tog with A.

ARGYLE LINES: Place D on wrong side of afghan. Pull lp through to right side at start of argyle line on chart, shown as fine line on chart.
* Insert hook down in next st or row, pull up lp and pull lp through lp on hook, repeat from * to end of line on chart. End off.

BORDER: Rnd 1: With A, work in sc around afghan, working 3 sc in each corner. Join; end off.

Rnds 2–6: With D, work sc in each sc around, 3 sc in each corner sc. Join each rnd.

Rnd 7: Working from left to right, sc in each sc around (crab st). Join; end off.

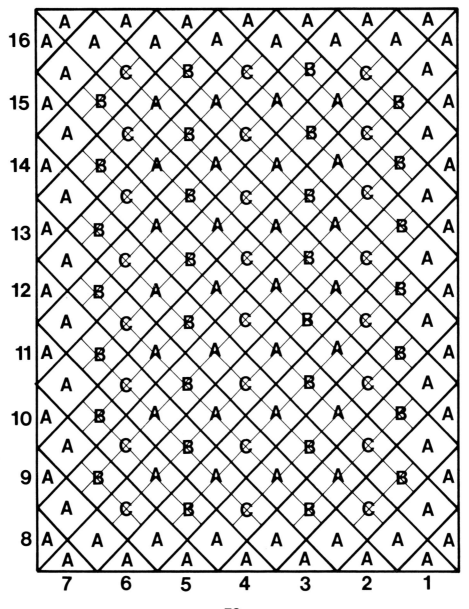

FOLK-ART TREE

A perennial folk-art favorite, the Tree of Life provides the perfect setting for other delightful folk motifs. All are cross-stitched in vibrant country colors on an afghan-stitch background.

For how-to information, see Afghan Basics at the back of the book.

SIZE:
54″ × 70″

MATERIALS:
Worsted-weight, 4-ply acrylic yarn (such as Brunswick Windrush): 38½ oz. Ecru, main color (MC); 10½ oz. Faded Denim Heather (A); 3½ oz. each Dark Goldenrod (B), Medium Gray Heather (C), Burgundy (D), and Strawberry Pink (E). Afghan hook size I (5.5 mm). Crochet hook size I, or size required to obtain correct gauge. Tapestry needle.

GAUGE:
13 sts = 3″; 11 rows = 3″.

AFGHAN STITCH:
Ch desired number of sts.

Row 1: Keeping all lps on hook, pull up a lp in 2nd ch from hook and in each ch across.

Work Off Lps: Yo hook, pull through first lp, * yo hook, pull through next 2 lps, repeat from * across until 1 lp remains on hook. Lp on hook counts as first st of next row.

Row 2: Keeping all lps on hook, sk first vertical bar, pull up a lp under next vertical bar and under each vertical bar across. Work off lps as before.

AFGHAN:

PANEL (make 3): With Ecru and afghan hook, ch 65. Work row 1 and row 2 of afghan stitch. Repeat row 2 until there are 240 rows. Sl st in 2nd vertical bar and in each bar across. Work 1 rnd of sc around panel, working 1 sc in each row and st, 2 sc in each corner. Sl st in first sc. End off.

EMBROIDERY: Side Panels:
Following chart 1, beg on 2nd row of panel and row 2 of chart, work design in cross-stitch to row 120, then repeat design from row 1 of chart, reversing B and C on bird.

Center Panel: Following chart 2, beg on 2nd row of panel and row 1 of chart, work design in cross-stitch to row 58. Following chart 1, work from row 1 to row 120, reversing B and C on bird. Following Chart 3, work from row 1 to row 50, then continue the 10 sts of tree trunk to top of afghan.

TO JOIN PANELS: Row 1: With A and crochet hook, ch 2; from right side, beg in lower right corner of left panel, work 3 dc in corner sc, * ch 1, sk 2 sc, 3 dc in next sc, repeat from * to top, end 3 dc in corner sc, ch 2. End off.

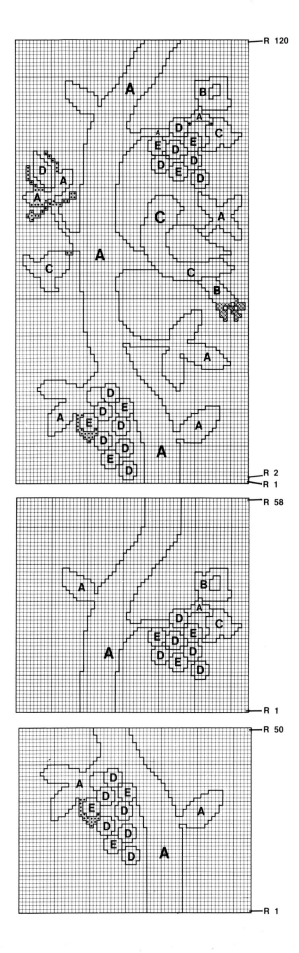

Row 2: Join D in first A ch at lower edge, ch 2; * 3 dc in next ch-1 sp, ch 1, repeat from * to top, end ch 1, sl st in 2nd ch of ch-2 at end of row 1. End off.

Row 3: Join A in corner sp at lower edge formed by A and D chs; ch 2; holding center panel along edge of left panel, sl st in corner sc of center panel; 2 dc in corner sp of left panel, * sk 2 sc of center panel, sl st in next sc, 3 dc in next sp of left panel, repeat from * to top, end 3 dc in top sp, sl st in corner of sc of center panel. End off.

Beginning at top edge of right panel, work 3 rows of shells as for left panel, joining to center panel on row 3.

BORDER: Rnd 1: From right side, join A in lower right corner of afghan; ch 2, 2 dc in same sc, * sk 2 sc, 3 dc in next sc, repeat from * to top, working 3 dc, ch 2, 3 dc in corner; repeat from * to * across top, working 3 dc in corner of panel, 3 dc in sp between panels, 3 dc in corner of next panel; continue in pat around, working 3 dc, ch 2, 3 dc in each corner, end ch 2, sl st in top of ch-2 at beg of rnd. End off.

Rnd 2: Join E in corner sp; ch 2, 2 dc, ch 2, 3 dc in corner sp; * 3 dc in next sp between shells, repeat from * around, working 3 dc, ch 2, 3 dc in each corner. Join; end off.

Rnd 3: Join D in corner sp; ch 2, 2 dc in sp, ch 3, sl st in last dc made for picot, 3 dc in corner sp, * ch 3, sl st in last dc, 3 dc in next sp, repeat from * around, working 3 dc, picot, 3 dc in each corner sp. Join; end off.

⊙ A   ⊠ B

QUICK-CROCHET GRANNY

Here is a contemporary version of the versatile and beloved American standby, worked in an unusual color combination.

For how-to information, see Afghan Basics at the back of the book.

SIZE:
45″ × 72″, plus fringe

MATERIALS:
Reynolds Lopi, 100-gram skeins, 5 skeins Gold (A), 6 skeins Bright Blue (B), 8 skeins Light Olive (C). Crochet hook size I, or size required to obtain correct gauge.

GAUGE:
8 sts = 3″. Each motif = 9″ square.

AFGHAN:

SQUARE (make 40): Beginning at center, with A, ch 4. Sl st in first ch to form ring.

Rnd 1: Ch 3, 2 dc in ring, (ch 3, 3 dc in ring) three times, ch 3, sl st in top of ch-3. End off.

Rnd 2: Join B in any ch-3 sp, ch 3, 2 dc in sp, ch 3, 3 dc in same sp, (ch 1, 3 dc, ch 3, 3 dc in next sp) three times, ch 1, sl st in top of ch-3. End off.

Rnd 3: Join C in any ch-3 corner sp, ch 3, 2 dc in sp, ch 3, 3 dc in same sp, (ch 1, 3 dc in next sp, ch 1, 3 dc, ch 3, 3 dc in next st) three times, ch 1, 3 dc in next sp, ch 1, sl st in top of ch-3. End off.

Rnd 4: With A, work as for rnd 3, having 1 more 3 dc group on each side.

Rnd 5: With B, work as for rnd 3, having 2 more 3 dc groups on each side.

Rnd 6: With C, work as for rnd 3, having 3 more 3 dc groups on each side.

FINISHING:
With C, sew squares tog, 5 squares by 8 squares, picking up back lp of each st around edge of each square. With C, work 1 rnd sc around edge of afghan, working sc in each dc, sc in each ch-1 sp, sc in each seam between motifs, and 3 sc in each corner of afghan.

FRINGE: Cut yarn 12″ long. Using 2 strands of one color tog, knot fringe in every other st on each end of afghan, alternating the 3 colors.

COLORGLOW

Easy single and double crochet leave the drama to the yarns in this versatile striped afghan. The combination of alternating off-white with variegated stripes achieves a lovely effect.

For how-to information, see Afghan Basics at the back of the book.

SIZE:

52″ × 66″, plus fringe

MATERIALS:

Worsted-weight, 4-ply yarn: 21 oz. Variegated or Ombre; 15 oz. Off-white. Crochet hook size l (5.5 mm), or size required to obtain correct gauge.

GAUGE:

4 sts = 1″.

AFGHAN:

With Off-white, ch 266.

Row 1: Sc in 2nd ch from hook, * ch 1, sk 1 ch, sc in next ch, repeat from * across. Ch 1, turn.

Row 2: Sc in first sc, * ch 1, sc in front lp of next sc, repeat from * across, end ch 1, sc in last sc. Ch 1, turn.

Rows 3–6: Repeat row 2. Cut Off-white. Join Variegated, ch 1, turn.

Rows 7–16: With Variegated, repeat row 2. Cut Variegated. Join Off-white, ch 1, turn.

Row 17: Repeat row 2. Ch 4, turn.

Row 18: Skip first sc and ch, * dc in front lp of next sc, ch 1, repeat from * across, end ch 1, dc in last sc. Ch 1, turn.

Row 19: Sc in first dc, * ch 1, sc in front lp of next dc, repeat from * across, end ch 1, sc in 3rd ch of ch-4. Cut Off-white. Join Variegated, ch 1, turn.

Repeat rows 7–19 for striped pattern seven times, then repeat rows 7–17. With Off-white, work in sc, ch 1, pattern for 5 rows. End off.

FRINGE: Cut yarn in 10″ lengths. Holding 3 strands tog, knot a fringe in every other row across short ends of afghan, matching stripes.

CORNER TO CORNER

Bold diagonal stripes in warm colors light up this charming knitted afghan. Using garter stitch, work from lower left diagonally across to the opposite corner.

For how-to information, see Afghan Basics at the back of the book.

SIZE:
40″ × 58″, plus fringe

MATERIALS:
Sport-weight, 3-ply acrylic yarn: 4 oz. each Brown (A), Copper (B), Gold (C), Old Gold (D), Honey (E); 2 oz. each Yellow (F), Burnt Orange (G). Circular needle No. 8, or size required to obtain correct gauge.

GAUGE:
4 sts = 1″; 8 rows (4 ridges) = 1″.

STRIPING PATTERN:
Working back and forth in garter st, work 10 rows each of A, B, C, D, E, F, E, D, C, B, A, G. Repeat these 120 rows for striping.

AFGHAN:
With A, cast on 3 sts.

Rows 1 and 2: Knit.

Row 3: Inc 1 st in each of first 2 sts, k 1—5 sts.

Row 4 and All Even Rows: K even.

Rows 5, 7, and 9: K, inc 1 st in first st, k to last 2 sts, inc 1 st in next st, k 1.

Row 10: K 11. Cut A.

Join B. Working in striping pat, repeat rows 5 and 4 alternately until there are 251 sts on needle, end with 10 rows of A. Continue in striping pattern as follows:

Row 1: K 1, k 2 tog, k to last 2 sts, inc 1 st in next st, k 1.

Row 2: K 251 sts. Repeat last 2 rows until 10 rows of 2nd B stripe in striping pattern have been completed. Continue to work in striping pattern as follows:

Row 1: K 1, k 2 tog, k to last 3 sts, k 2 tog, k 1.

Row 2: Knit. Repeat last 2 rows until 3 sts remain. Bind off.

FINISHING:

FRINGE: Cut strands of yarn 10″ long. Using 1 strand of each color tog, knot fringe in every color change across top and bottom edges. Trim ends. Steam lightly.

COZY ARAN

Textured knitting patterns native to Ireland's Aran Islands continue to be very popular. This winning design repeats a combination of three authentic motifs.

For how-to information, see Afghan Basics at the back of the book.

SIZE:
66″ × 78″

MATERIALS:
Worsted-weight, 4-ply yarn: 42 oz. Off-white. Knitting needles No. 8 (5 mm), or size required to obtain correct gauge. Crochet hook size H (5 mm). Double-pointed needle. Tapestry needle.

GAUGE:
4 sts = 1″; 6 rows = 1″ (reverse stockinette st).

SPECIAL ABBREVIATIONS:
K1b: K into back of st.

Rc st: Right cross stitch. With dp needle, sl next st and hold in back of work, k next st, then p st from dp needle.

Lc st: Left cross stitch. With dp needle, sl next st and hold in front of work, p next st, then k st from dp needle.

Rt st: Right twist stitch. With dp needle, sl next st and hold in back of work, k next 2 sts, then p st from dp needle.

Lt st: Left twist stitch. With dp needle, sl next 2 sts and hold in front of work, k next st, then k 2 sts from dp needle.

PATTERN STITCHES:

PATTERN 1 (worked on even number of sts):

Row 1: * K 1, p 1, repeat from * across.

Row 2: * P 1, k 1, repeat from * across.

Repeat these 2 rows for pat 1.

PATTERN 2 (worked on 6 sts):

Row 1 (right side): P 2, sl next 2 sts to dp needle and hold in back, k 2, k 2 sts from dp needle (cable twist made), p 2.

Row 2: K 2, p 4, k 2.

Row 3: P 2, k 4, p 2.

Row 4: Repeat row 2.

Repeat these 4 rows for pat 2.

PATTERN 3 (worked on 17 sts):

Row 1 (right side): P 7, k3b, p 7.

Rows 2 and All Even Rows: K the k sts and p the p sts.

Row 3: P 6, rc st on next 2 sts, k1b, lc st on next 2 sts, p 6.

Row 5: P 5, rc st, p 1, k1b, p 1, lc st, p 5.

Row 7: P 4, rc st, p 2, k1b, p 2, lc st, p 4.

Row 9: P 3, rc st, p 3, k1b, p 3, lc st, p 3.

Row 11: P 2, rc st, p 4, k1b, p 4, lc st, p 2.

Row 13: P 1, rc st, p 4, k3b, p 4, lc st, p 1.

Row 14: Work as for all even rows.

Repeat rows 3–14 for pat 3 (12-row repeat).

PATTERN 4 (worked on 20 sts):

Row 1 (right side): P 8, with dp needle sl next 2 sts and hold in back of work, k 2, k 2 from dp needle, p 8.

Rows 2 and All Even Rows: K the k sts and p the p sts.

Row 3: P 7, rt st on next 3 sts, lt st on next 3 sts, p 7.

Row 5: P 6, rt st, (p 1, k 1) once, lt st, p 6.

Row 7: P 5, rt st, (p1, k 1) twice, lt st, p 5.

Row 9: P 4, rt st, (p 1, k 1) 3 times, lt st, p 4.

Row 11: P 3, rt st, (p 1, k 1) 4 times, lt st, p 3.

Row 13: P 2, rt st, (p 1, k 1) 5 times, lt st, p 2.

Row 15: P 1, rt st, (p 1, k 1) 6 times, lt st, p 1.

Row 17: P 1, k 2, (k 1, p 1) 7 times, k 2, p 1.

Row 19: P 1, lt st, (k1, p 1) 6 times, rt st, p 1.

Row 21: P 2, lt st, (k 1, p 1) 5 times, rt st, p 2.

Row 23: P 3, lt st, (k 1, p 1) 4 times, rt st, p 3.

Row 25: P 4, lt st, (k 1, p 1) 3 times, rt st, p 4.

Row 27: P 5, lt st, (k 1, p 1) twice, rt st, p 5.

Row 29: P 6, lt st, (k 1, p 1) once, rt st, p 6.

Row 31: P 7, lt st, rt st, p 7.

Row 32: Work as for all even rows. Repeat rows 1–32 for pat 4.

AFGHAN:

PANEL (make 3): Beginning at lower edge, cast on 84 sts. Work 5 rows of pat 1.

Row 1 (right side): Work row 1 of pat 1 across next 4 sts, k1b, work row 1 of pat 2 across next 6 sts, k1b, work row 1 of pat 3 across next 17 sts, k1b p 1, k1b, work row 1 of pat 4 across next 20 sts, k1b, p 1, k1b, work row 1 of pat 3 across next 17 sts, k1b, work row 1 of pat 2 across next 6 sts, k1b, work row 1 of pat 1 across last 4 sts.

Row 2 and All Even Rows: K the k sts and p the p sts for all pats except pat 1 (p the k sts and k the p sts).

Repeat last 2 rows, working and repeating the 2 rows of pat 1, the 4 rows of pat 2, the 12 rows of pat 3 and the 32 rows of pat 4, until pat 4 has been worked nine times, end 5 rows of pat 1 across all sts; bind off loosely in pat.

FINISHING:

From wrong side, weave panels tog, matching rows.

BORDER: From right side, work 1 sc in each k st across cast-on edge of afghan. Do not turn.

Row 2: Ch 1, working from left to right, sc in each sc (crab st, see page 182). End off.

Work same border on bound-off edge of afghan.

OCTAGON MOSAIC

This is a great lap project as octagons are worked separately, then squared off with corner triangles and sewn together. Soft, heathery colors capture the country mood.

For how-to information, see Afghan Basics at the back of the book.

SIZE:
48″ × 64″

MATERIALS:
Bulky-weight yarn: 14 oz. each Burgundy and Denim Blue, 10½ oz. each Off-white, Bright Blue, Blue-pink Heather, Gray-blue, Light Burgundy, and Green. Crochet hook size K (6.5 mm), or size required to obtain correct gauge. Pillow forms, 16″ square. Fabric, ½ yd. for each pillow.

GAUGE:
1 octagon = 8″.

AFGHAN:

OCTAGONS: With A, ch 5. Sl st in first ch to form ring.

Rnd 1: With A, ch 3 (always counts as first dc), 15 dc in ring, sl st in top of ch-3—16 sts. End off.

Rnd 2: Join B, ch 3, 2 dc in base of ch 3, * dc in next dc, 3 dc in next dc, repeat from * six times, dc in next dc, sl st in top of ch-3—32 sts. End off.

Rnd 3: Join C, ch 3, * 3 dc in next dc, dc in 3 dc, repeat from * six times, 3 dc in next dc, dc in next 2 dc, sl st in top of ch-3—48 sts. End off.

Rnd 4: Join D, ch 3, dc in next dc, * 3 dc in next dc, dc in 5 dc, repeat from * six times, 3 dc in next dc, dc in 3 dc, sl st in top of ch-3—64 sts. End off.

Make a total of 48 octagons, 8 each in the following color combinations:

#1: A Light Burgundy, B Off-white, C Green, D Bright Blue.

#2: A Green, B Light Burgundy, C Blue-pink, D Burgundy.

#3: A Denin Blue, B Burgundy, C Gray-blue, D Blue-pink.

#4: A Gray-blue, B Bright Blue, C Burgundy, D Denim Blue.

#5: Bright Blue, B Blue-pink, C Denim Blue, D Off-white.

#6: A Blue-pink, B Bright Blue, C Off-white, D Green.

#7: A Burgundy, B Gray-blue, C Denim Blue, D Light Burgundy.

#8: A Off-white, B Green, C Light Burgundy, D Gray-blue.

TRIANGLES: Row 1: Following chart, join indicated color to 3rd dc of 3-dc cluster, ch 1, sc in 7 dc. Ch 1, turn each row.

Row 2: Dec 1 sc, sc in 5 dc, dec 1 sc.

Row 3: Dec 1 sc, sc in 3 dc, dec 1 sc.

Row 4: Dec 1 sc, sc in next sc, dec 1 sc.

Row 5: Draw up a lp in remaining 3 sc, yo and pull through 4 lps on hook. End off. Work triangles onto

AFGHAN: *(continued)*

octagons as shown on chart in
the following colors.
- **#9:** Off-white.
- **#10:** Bright Blue.
- **#11:** Blue-pink
- **#12:** Gray-blue.
- **#13:** Light Burgundy.
- **#14:** Green.
- **#15:** Denim Blue.

FINISHING:

Sew squares tog following chart.
With A, work 1 row sc around
entire afghan. End off.

PILLOW #1:

With Off-white, ch 5. Sl st in first
ch to form ring.

Rnds 1 and 2: Repeat octagon #8
rnds 1 and 2. End off.

Rnds 3 and 4: Join Green, repeat
octagon #8 rnds 3 and 4. End off.

Rnd 5: Join Light Burgundy, ch 3,
dc in 2 dc, * 3 dc in next dc, dc
in 7 dc, repeat from * six times, 3
dc in next dc, dc in 4 dc, sl st
in top of ch-3—80 sts.

Rnd 6: Ch 3, dc in 3 dc, * 3 dc in
next dc, dc in 9 dc, repeat from
* six times, 3 dc in next dc, dc in 5
dc, sl st in top of ch-3—96 sts.
End off.

Rnd 7: Join Gray-blue, ch 3, dc in
4 dc, * 3 dc in next dc, dc in 11
dc, repeat from * six times, 3 dc in
next dc, dc in 6 dc, sl st in top
of ch-3—112 sts.

Rnd 8: Ch 3, dc in 5 dc, * 3 dc in
next dc, dc in 13 dc, repeat from
* six times, 3 dc in next dc, dc in 7
dc, sl st in top of ch-3—128 sts.
End off.

TRIANGLES: Row 1: Beginning at 3rd
dc of 3-dc cluster, attach 1 of 4
remaining colors, ch 1, sc in 18 sc.
Ch 1, turn. Continue in sc, dec 1
st each edge every row 6 times. End
off as on afghan triangles.

PILLOW #2:

Work as for pillow #1 following
colors of octagon #4.

PILLOW #3:

LARGE TRIANGLE: With Denim,
ch 36.

Row 1: Sc in 2nd ch from hook and
in each ch across. Ch 1, turn.
Continue in sc, dec 1 st each edge
of every row until 3 sts remain.
End off as on afghan triangle. Make
three more large triangles with
Blue-pink, Off-white, and Bright Blue.
Sew these 4 triangles tog to form
a square.

FINISHING:

TO MAKE PILLOW: Cut out pillow front from fabric, 17″ square. Cut pillow back same size. With right sides together, stitch pillow front and back together, making ½″ seams and leaving an opening in one side for turning. Turn pillow to right side. Insert pillow form. Turn in raw edges and slip-stitch opening closed.

Sew pillow top to front of pillow.

ASSEMBLY DIAGRAM

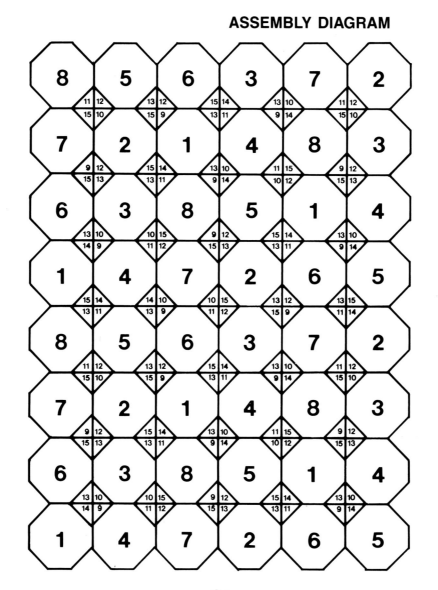

PINWHEELS

Catch the breezes with this colorful knit pattern of playful eyelet pinwheels set in bold stripes.

For how-to information, see Afghan Basics at the back of the book.

SIZE:
45½″ × 56½″

MATERIALS:
Worsted-weight, 4-ply yarn: 10½ oz. each Coral (A), and Yellow (B); 7 oz. each Purple (C), and Blue (D). Circular knitting needles, 29″ long, Nos. 6 and 8 (4.25 mm and 5 mm), or size required to obtain correct gauge.

GAUGE:
18 sts = 4″; 24 rows = 4″.

SPECIAL ABBREVIATION:
Ssk: Sl 2 sts knitwise to right-hand needle, insert left-hand needle into front of these sts and k them tog.

PATTERN STITCH:

PINWHEEL PATTERN (worked on 21 sts):
Row 1 and All Wrong-Side Rows: Purl.
Row 2: K 12, k 2 tog, yo, k 7.
Row 4: K 11, k 2 tog, yo, k 8.
Row 6: K 10, (k 2 tog, yo) twice, k 7.
Row 8: K 9, (k 2 tog, yo) twice, k 8.
Row 10: K 8, (k 2 tog, yo) 3 times, k 7.
Row 12: K 2, (yo, ssk) twice, yo, sl 1, k 2 tog, psso, yo, (k 2 tog, yo) twice, k 1, yo, ssk, k 5.
Row 14: K 3, (yo, ssk) twice, k 1, (k 2 tog, yo) twice, k 3, yo, ssk, k 4.
Row 16: K 4, yo, ssk, yo, sl 1, k 2 tog, psso, yo, (k 2 tog, yo) twice, k 1, (yo, ssk) twice, k 3.
Row 18: K 5, yo, ssk, k 1, (k 2 tog, yo) twice, k 3 (yo, ssk) twice, k 2.
Row 20: K 6, yo, sl 1, k 2 tog, psso, yo, (k 2 tog, yo) twice, k 1, (yo, ssk) 3 times, k 1.
Row 22: K 6 (k 2 tog, yo) 3 times, k 9.
Row 24: K 7, (k 2 tog, yo) twice, k 10.
Row 26: K 6, (k 2 tog, yo) twice, k 11.
Row 28: K 7, k 2 tog, yo, k 12.
Row 30: K 6, k 2 tog, yo, k 13.
Row 31: Repeat row 1. Repeat rows 1–31 for pinwheel pat.

AFGHAN:
With smaller needles and C, cast on 204 sts. Work in garter st (k each row) for 1½″. Change to large needles. ** With D, k 2 rows. Change to B.
Next Row (right side): Knit.
Row 1 and All Wrong-Side Rows: * P 6, k 3, pinwheel pat row 1 across 21 sts, k 3, repeat from * across, end p 6.
Row 2: K 6, * p 3, pinwheel pat row 2 across 21 sts, p 3, k 6, repeat from * across.
Row 4: P 6, * p 3, pinwheel pat row 4 across next 21 sts, p 9, repeat from * across. Repeat rows 1–4 seven times, rows 1–3 once for each stripe, working consecutive pinwheel pat rows. With C, k 2 rows. Change to A.

Next Row (right side): Knit. With A, work a stripe as above. With B, k 2 rows. Change to D.

Next Row (right side): Knit. With D, work a stripe as above. With A, k 2 rows. Change to C.

Next Row (right side): Knit. With C, work a stripe as above. ** Repeat from ** to ** until 10 stripes have been completed. With B, k 2 rows. With C, work in garter st for 1½". Bind off.

PATTERNS WITH PIZAZZ

An unusual collection of striking designs—most are easy to do, and many can be made right from your box of leftover yarns. Bold splashes of color appear in Add A Strip, an easy crochet project that begins around a center square and builds strip-by-strip to a full-sized rug. Borrowed from a traditional patchwork pattern, Log Cabin is knit in garter-stitch strips of alternating light and dark colors. Two dazzling step patterns—one wide, one narrow—will appeal to crocheters, as will Picnic Plaid, where the plaid is woven in contrasting colors on a crocheted mesh foundation. For spectacular effects with subtle shading, try the easy and popular crochet Sunset Ripple, or if you're up for a challenge, the magnificent Blue Star "Quilt."

opposite page: *Add A Strip*

ADD A STRIP

With the easy add-a-strip technique, create this bold, vibrant afghan. The overall size can be varied simply by adding bands of color.

For how-to information, see Afghan Basics at the back of the book.

SIZE:
50″ square

MATERIALS:
Worsted-weight, 4-ply yarn: 1 oz. Black (A); 2 oz. each Royal (B), Periwinkle Blue (C), Pale Blue (D), and White (E); 4 oz. Wine Red (F); 5 oz. Red (G); 6 oz. Pink (H); 4 oz. each Coral (I) and Orange (J); 5 oz. Yellow (K); 9 oz. Mauve (L); 3 oz. Pale Pink (M). Crochet hook size G (4.25 mm), or size required to obtain correct gauge.

GAUGE:
4 sc = 1″; 4 rows = 1″.

AFGHAN:
Beginning at center, with Black, ch 21.

Row 1: Sc in 2nd ch from hook and in each ch—20 sc. Ch 1, turn each row.

Rows 2–20: Sc in each sc. End off. Piece should measure 5″ square.

Row 21 (right side): Join Royal at lower right edge of piece. Working up right edge, sc in each row to top working sc, ch 2, sc in top corner, sc in each sc across top—20 sc on 2 sides, ch 2 sp at corner. Ch 1, turn.

Rows 22–30: Sc in each sc, sc, ch 2, sc in ch-2 sp at corner. Ch 1, turn each row. End off.

Row 31 (right side): From right side, join Periwinkle in first st of row 30. Sc in 10 rows of Royal, sc in 20 rows of Black working sc, ch 2, sc in lower corner, sc in each ch across starting ch, sc in 10 rows of Royal. Ch 1, turn.

Rows 32–40: Sc in each sc, sc, ch 2, sc in ch-2 sp at corner. Ch 1, turn each row. End off.

Continue in this manner, working 10 rows of sc on 2 sides of piece, working sc, ch 2, sc in corner sp each row. Always start new color on right side of afghan and work on the 2 sides opposite to the last 2 sides worked. Follow diagram for colors.

When 10 rows of Yellow have been worked, work each corner of afghan separately as follows:

Row 1 (right side): Join Mauve in first st on one side of afghan, dec 1 sc (pull up a lp in first and 2nd sts, yo and through 3 lps on hook), sc in 65 sc changing to Pale Pink in last sc; finish row with Pale Pink, dec 1 sc at end of row. Ch 1, turn.

Rows 2–10: Continue in established colors, dec 1 st each end every row.

Row 11: With Pink, dec 1 sc, work 50 sc, finish row with Wine Red, dec 1 sc at end of row.

Rows 12–20: Continue in established colors, dec 1 st each end every row.

Following chart, continue to work 10 rows of 2 colors, dec 1 sc at each end every row. Work remaining sts in Black.

FINISHING:

With Mauve, work 6 rows of sc around afghan, working sc, ch 2, sc in each corner each row. Join each row.

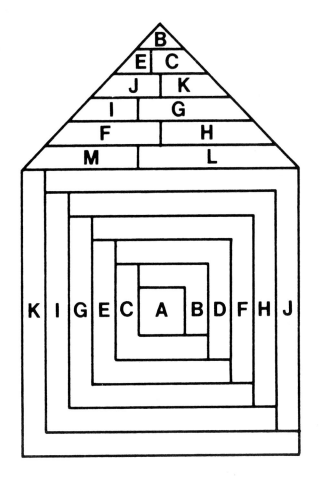

COLOR-CHROME WIDE STEPS

Carefully placed colors and raised stitches give this dazzling afghan its three-dimensional look. It is worked in single crochet with a double-crochet overlay.

For how-to information, see Afghan Basics at the back of the book.

SIZE:
45″ × 60″

MATERIALS:
Worsted-weight, 4-ply yarn: 7 oz. Light Olive; 6 oz. Medium Lavender; 5 oz. each Off-white and Medium Orange; 4 oz. each Dark Brown, Light Blue, Shaded Blues, Pale Yellow, Bright Pink, Dark Rust, and Shaded Sandtones; 3 oz. each Warm Beige, Light Burnt Orange, Bright Rose; 2 oz. each Terracotta, Dark Blue, Black, Bright Red, Medium Brown, Lilac, Shaded Browns, Dark Gold, Dark Skipper Blue, Bright Yellow. Crochet hook size F (3.75 mm), or size required to obtain correct gauge.

GAUGE:
9 sts = 2″; 4 rows = 1″.

AFGHAN:
Beginning at long edge and leaving 6″ end, with Dark Brown, ch 267, having 9 ch sts to 2″.

Row 1 (right side): 2 sc in 2nd ch from hook, sc in each ch to last ch, 2 sc in last ch—268 sc. Ch 1 to fasten. Leaving 6″ end, cut strand and pull end through lp. Do not turn.

Row 2: Leaving 6″ end, with Dark Brown, make lp on hook, sk first sc, 2 sc in next sc (selvedge made at beg of row); sc in back lp of each sc across to last 2 sc, sk next sc, 2 sc in both lps of last sc (selvedge made at end of row). Ch 1; cut as before. Do not turn.

Note: Start and end each row in same way as before, leaving 6″ ends. Always work from right side.

Row 3: Make selvedge, sc in back lp of next 4 sc; mark last 2 sc worked; * sc in back lp of next 10 sc, mark last 2 sc worked; repeat from * to last 12 sc, sc in back lp of next 10 sc, make selvedge.

Rows 4 and 5: Repeat row 2.

Row 6: With Pale Yellow, make selvedge, sc in back lp of next 2 sc; yo, draw up a lp in front lp of first marked sc 3 rows below and draw lp to height of row in work, (yo and through 2 lps) twice

(raised dc made); make a raised dc in front lp of next marked sc 3 rows below, * sk the 2 sc behind raised dc's, sc in back lp of next 8 sc, make a raised dc in front lp of each of next 2 marked sc; repeat from * to last 12 sc, sc in back lp of next 10 sc, make selvedge.

Row 7: Make selvedge, sc in back lp of next 2 sc, * sc in back lp of 2 raised dc, (raised dc in front lp of next sc 3 rows below) twice, sk the 2 sc behind raised dc's, sc in back lp of next 6 sc, repeat from * twenty-five more times; sc in back lp of next 2 sc; make selvedge.

Hereafter, to move the raised dc pat as before, work raised dc groups 1 row higher than raised dc groups on previous row and in front lp of next 2 sts to the left. Always sk 2 sc behind each group of raised dc's and work each sc in back lp of st, except for selvedges.

Row 8: Make selvedge, 4 sc, mark last 2 sc worked, make 2 more sc, 2 raised dc, (8 sc, 2 raised dc) twenty-five times, 6 sc, selvedge.

Row 9: With Light Olive, make selvedge, (8 sc, 2 raised dc) twenty-six times, 4 sc, selvedge.

Row 10: Make selvedge, 10 sc, 2 raised dc, (8 sc, 2 raised dc) twenty-five times, 2 sc, selvedge.

Row 11: Make selvedge, 2 sc, raised dc in front lp of each of 2 marked sts 3 rows below, (8 sc, 2 raised dc) twenty-five times, 2 sc, selvedge.

Repeating rows 7–11 for stitch pat, work the following number of rows of color: 3 Medium Lavender, 2 Terracotta, 1 Light Burnt Orange, 2 Dark Blue, 1 Black, 3 each Light Blue, Bright Red, Off-white, Medium Brown, Medium Orange, Warm Beige, Shaded Blues, Bright Pink, Pale Yellow, and Light Olive; 2 Medium Lavender; 1 each Lilac, Light Burnt Orange, Terracotta, Medium Orange, Shaded Browns, Dark Rust, Shaded Browns, Dark Blue; 2 Black; 3 each Light Blue, Dark Rust, Off-white, Bright Rose, Shaded Sandtones, Light Olive, Medium Lavender, and Medium Orange; 2 Warm Beige; 1 Shaded Sandtones; 3 each Shaded Blues, Bright Pink, Lilac, Pale Yellow, Dark Rust, and Bright Rose; 2 Dark Gold; 1 Pale Yellow; 3 each Light Olive, Medium Lavender, Medium Orange, Shaded Sandtones, Dark Skipper Blue, and Light Blue; 1 each Light Burnt Orange, Bright Red, and Bright Rose; 3 Off-white; 2 Medium Brown; 1 Dark Rust; 3 each of Shaded Sandtones, Light Olive, Medium Lavender, and Medium Orange; 1 Warm Beige; 2 Dark Gold; 2 Dark Skipper Blue; 1 Dark Blue; 3 each Shaded Blues, Light Burnt Orange, Bright Pink, and Off-white; 1 Shaded Browns; 1 Dark Rust, 1 Shaded Browns; 3 each of Light Olive, Bright Yellow, and Dark Brown.

Last 2 Rows: With Dark Brown, make selvedge, 264 sc and selvedge.

FRINGE: Beg at corner, pick up ends of first 5 rows, make a knot close to edge of afghan. Cut a 12″ length of yarn matching color of next 3 rows; draw half the length through center end st of next 3 rows—5 strands. Knot strands tog as before. Continue to knot 5 strands tog every 3 rows to opposite corner. Trim.

COLOR-CHROME NARROW STEPS

Another dazzling step pattern in single crochet with a double-crochet overlay. It is worked from end to end, leaving excess for a long self-fringe.

For how-to information, see Afghan Basics at the back of the book.

SIZE:
46″ × 64″

MATERIALS:
Worsted-weight, 4-ply acrylic yarn: 7 oz. each Black and Eggshell; 3½ oz. each of Light Rust, Dark Skipper Blue, Warm Beige, Bright Yellow-Green, Medium Blue, Taupe; 4 oz. each Bright Rose, Bright Orange, Dark Brown, Medium Lavender, Bright Red, Lilac, Emerald Green, Bright Yellow, and Bright Pink. Crochet hook size F (3.75 mm), or size required to obtain correct gauge.

GAUGE:
7 sts = 2″; 4 rows = 1″.

AFGHAN:
Beginning at long edge and leaving 12″ end, with Dark Skipper Blue, ch 223, having 7 ch sts to 2″.

Row 1 (right side): Sc in 2nd ch from hook, * sc in next 10 ch; mark last sc worked; repeat from * to last ch, sc in last ch—222 sts. Ch 1 to fasten. Leaving a 12″ end, cut strand and pull end through lp. Do not turn.

Row 2: Leaving a 12″ end, with Bright Rose, make lp on hook; beg in first sc of last row, sc in each sc across. Fasten off and cut 12″ end as before.

Note: Start and end each row in same way, leaving 12″ ends. Always work from right side.

Row 3: With Medium Lavender, sc in each sc across.

Row 4: With Bright Orange, sc in first 10 sc; yo, insert hook from right to left under bar of next marked sc 3 rows below and draw up a lp to height of row in work, (yo and through 2 lps) twice (raised dc made); * sk sc behind raised dc, sc in next 9 sc, raised dc in next marked sc on 3rd row below; repeat from * to last sc, sk sc behind raised dc, sc in last sc.

Hereafter, to move raised dc pat diagonally, work raised dc's 1 row higher than raised dc's of previous row (3 rows below in work) and 1 st to the right. Always sk sc behind raised dc.

Row 5: With Light Rust, (make 9 sc, 1 raised dc) twenty-two times, 2 sc.

Row 6: With Lilac, make 8 sc, 1 raised dc, (9 sc, 1 raised dc) twenty-one times, 3 sc.

Row 7: With Warm Beige, make 7 sc, 1 raised dc, (9 sc, 1 raised dc) twenty-one times, 4 sc.

Row 8: With Bright Red, sk first sc, make 5 sc, 1 raised dc, (9 sc, 1 raised dc) twenty-one times, 4 sc, 2 sc in last sc—222 sts.

Row 9: With Dark Brown, make 4 sc, 1 raised dc, (9 sc, 1 raised dc) twenty-one times, 7 sc.

Row 10: With Emerald Green, make 3 sc, 1 raised dc, (9 sc, 1 raised dc) twenty-one times, 7 sc; mark last sc worked; make 1 more sc.

Row 11: With Taupe, make 2 sc, 1 raised dc, (9 sc, 1 raised dc) twenty-one times, 9 sc.

Row 12: With Eggshell, make 1 sc, 1 raised dc, (9 sc, 1 raised dc) twenty-one times, 10 sc.

Row 13: With Black, make 10 sc, 1 raised dc, (9 sc, 1 raised dc) twenty times, 9 sc, raised dc in marked sc, 1 sc.

Rows 5–13 form pat stitch. Work until piece is 46″ long, using Black for every 11th row and Eggshell either for the row below or above Black, changing colors for other rows at random.

EDGING: With Black, sc in each st across; turn. Sl st in each sc across. End off. Work same edging on opposite edge, working in each ch of starting ch.

FINISHING:

Pin to measurements, dampen and let dry.

FRINGE: Row 1: Beginning at corner, knot first 6 strands tog 1″ below edge of afghan. Knot each 6 strands tog across edge.

Row 2: Knot first 3 strands of first fringe tog 1″ below first knot, Knot remaining 3 strands tog with 3 strands of next fringe. Continue in this way across for 2nd row of knots. Trim fringe.

PICNIC PLAID

This fresh-as-summer afghan has a white mesh background with bold stripes crocheted in. The colorful plaid is later woven in with a blunt needle.

For how-to information, see Afghan Basics at the back of the book.

SIZE:

52″ × 58″, plus fringe

MATERIALS:

Worsted-weight, 4-ply yarn: 35 oz. Off-white (A); 7 oz. Light Olive (B); 10½ oz. Bright Pink (C); 3½ oz. each Light Blue (D) and Light Burnt Orange (E). Crochet hook size J, or size required to obtain correct gauge. J. & P. Coats candlewick needle or bodkin.

GAUGE:

4 sts = 1″; 6 rows = 2″.

PATTERN STITCH:

Row 1: Hdc in 5th ch from hook, * ch 1, sk 1 ch, hdc in next ch, repeat from * across. Ch 3, turn.

Row 2: Sk first hdc, hdc in next hdc, * ch 1, hdc in next hdc, repeat from * across, end ch 1, sk 1 ch of turning ch, hdc in next ch. Ch 3, turn.

AFGHAN:

Beginning at lower edge, with A, ch 211. Work row 1 of pat st—104 sps plus ch-3. Work row 2 of pat st. Repeat row 2 for afghan. Cut and join colors as needed.

STRIPED PATTERN: Work 5 rows A, * 2 rows B, 4 rows C, 3 rows A, 2 rows D, 14 rows A; repeat from * 6 times, ending last repeat with only 4 rows A. There should be 7 color stripes.

WEAVING: Cut strands of yarn 24″ longer than length of afghan. Thread 3 strands of A in needle or bodkin.

Line 1: Leaving 10″ free for fringe at bottom edge, and working through end sps at right edge of afghan, bring yarn from back to front in bottom sp, * from front to back in sp above, from back to front in sp above, repeat from * to top of afghan, leaving 10″ free at top for fringe.

Line 2: With 3 strands of A in needle, leaving 10″ free at bottom edge, bring yarn from front to back in next bottom sp, * from back to front in sp above, from front to back in sp above, repeat from * to top of afghan. Continue to weave yarn in this manner through each line of sps alternating lines 1 and 2. Weave 2 more lines of A.

Color Stripes: * Weave 2 lines B, 2 lines C, 1 line B, 2 lines E, 1 line B, 14 lines A, repeat from * across, end 4 lines A.

FRINGE: Knot each 6 ends tog across top and bottom of afghan. Trim fringe.

LOG CABIN

Log Cabin is a beloved quilt pattern, adapted here for knitting. It makes an unusual afghan with striking graphic appeal—and a perfect project for using up yarn scraps.

For how-to information, see Afghan Basics at the back of the book.

SIZE:
36" × 50"

MATERIALS:
Worsted-weight, 4-ply yarn: 6 oz. Red, main color, 12 oz. of light colors, and 12 oz. of dark colors. (Use colors you have on hand; have at least 4 light shades and 4 dark shades. The more shades you use, the better your afghan will look). Knitting needles No. 8. Circular knitting needle No. 8, or size required to obtain correct gauge.

GAUGE:
9 sts = 2". Each square = 7".

PATTERN STITCH:
GARTER STITCH: Row 1: Knit.
Row 2: Knit. Repeat rows 1 and 2 for garter stitch.

AFGHAN:
SQUARE (make 35):
First Section: With Red, cast on 8 sts. K 16 rows (8 ridges). Cut yarn; sl these 8 sts to a thread.
2nd Section: With first dark color, pick up and k 8 sts (1 st for each ridge) along left side of Red square. K 11 more rows. Sl these 8 sts to a thread.

3rd Section: With 2nd dark color, pick up and k 6 sts along left side of dark section and 8 sts along cast-on edge of Red square. K 11 more rows. Sl these 14 sts to a thread.

4th Section: With first light color, pick up and k 6 sts along left side of 3rd section and 8 sts along 3rd side of Red square. K 11 more rows. Sl these 14 sts to a thread.

5th Section: With 2nd light color, pick up and k 6 sts along left side of 4th section, 8 sts from thread of Red square and 6 sts from right side of first dark section. K 11 more rows. Sl these 20 sts to a thread.

6th Section: With 3rd dark color, pick up and k 6 sts along left side of 5th section, 8 sts from thread of first dark section and 6 sts along right side of 2nd dark section. K 10 more rows on these 20 sts. Bind off.

7th Section: With 4th dark color, pick up and k 6 sts along left side of 6th section, 14 sts from thread of 2nd dark section and 6 sts along right side of first light section. K 10 more rows on these 26 sts. Bind off.

8th Section: With 3rd light color, pick up and k 6 sts along left side of 7th section, 14 sts from thread of first light section, and 6 sts along side of 2nd light section. K 10 more rows on these 26 sts. Bind off.

9th Section: With 4th light color, pick up and k 6 sts along left side of 8th section, 20 sts from thread of 2nd light section and 6 sts along side of 3rd dark section. K 10 more rows on these 32 sts. Bind off.

FINISHING:

Run in yarn ends on wrong side. Arrange squares as shown in picture; sew tog. (For larger afghan, with more squares, experiment with other arrangements, or consult a quilt book.)

BORDER: From right side, with Red and circular needle, pick up and k 1 st for each st or ridge along one side of afghan, about 32 sts per square. Work back and forth on these sts as follows:

Row 1 (wrong side): K 1, inc 1 st in next st, k to 2 sts from end, inc 1 st in next st, k 1.

Row 2: K.

Row 3: Repeat row 1. Bind off in p on right side. Work 3 remaining sides the same. Sew corners.

BLUE STAR "QUILT"

A quilter's Broken Star pattern becomes a crocheter's dream in this fabulous afghan. Four shades of blue dramatically enhance the traditional blue-and-white design.

For how-to information, see Afghan Basics at the back of the book.

SIZE:
71″ × 66″, plus fringe

MATERIALS:
Worsted-weight, 4-ply acrylic yarn: 70 oz. Eggshell (MC); 10½ oz. Cadet Blue (A); 7 oz. each White (B), Light Blue (C), Robin Blue (D), and Colonial Blue (E). Afghan and crochet hooks size H (5 mm), or size required to obtain correct gauge. Tapestry needle.

GAUGE:
16 sts = 4″; 16 rows = 4″.

AFGHAN STITCH:
Ch the desired number of sts.

Row 1: Draw up a lp in 2nd ch from hook and in each ch across.

To Work Lps Off: Yo and pull through 1 lp, * yo and pull through 2 lps, repeat from * across. Lp that remains on hook counts as first st of next row.

Row 2: Draw up a lp in 2nd vertical bar and in each vertical bar across. Work lps off as before. Repeat row 2 for afghan st.

Finishing Row: * Pull up a lp under vertical bar and through the lp in hook, repeat from * across. End off.

AFGHAN:

SIDE PANEL (make 2): With afghan hook and Eggshell, ch 91. Work in afghan st for 255 rows. Work finishing row.

CENTER PANEL (make 1): With afghan hook and Eggshell, ch 100. Work in afghan st for 255 rows. Work finishing row.

FINISHING:
Sew side panels to center panel. Joined edges count as 1 stitch in embroidery, not 2.

EMBROIDERY: Beginning at lower corner of afghan, following chart, embroider motif in cross-stitch, working from A to B once, from B to A once. The C line is where the crocheted panels meet. Work to row 128. Turn chart upside down, continue embroidery, beg with row 127.

EDGING: With crochet hook and A, work 4 rnds sc around afghan, working 3 sc in each corner. Change to Eggshell, work 1 rnd sc. End off.

FRINGE: Using four 11″ lengths of MC for each fringe, fold lengths in half. With right side of afghan facing, pull center of fringe from front to back through corner sc at lower right edge of afghan forming a lp, pull ends of fringe through lp and tighten. Sk next sc, make a fringe in next st, continue to make fringes in every other st as established on upper and lower edges of afghan.

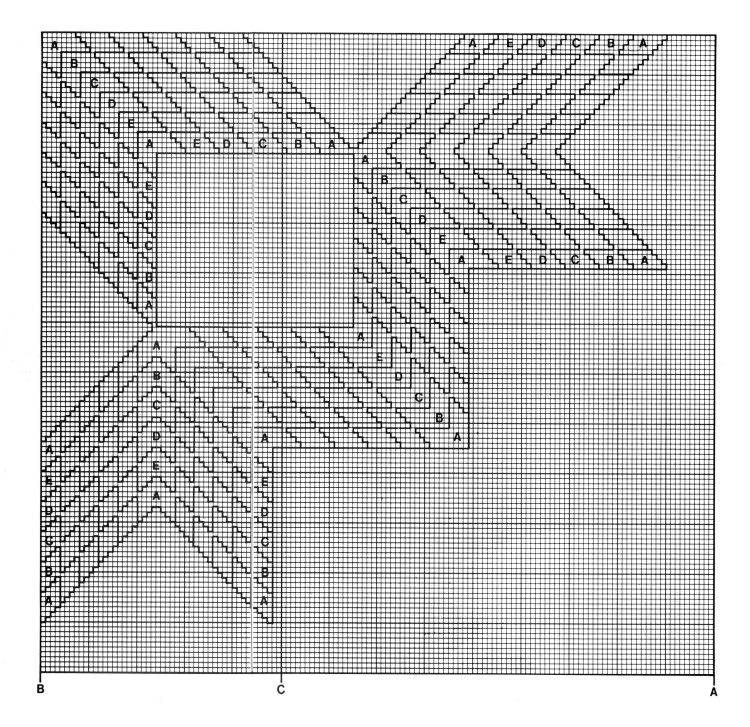

SUNSET RIPPLE

Crocheted in an all-time favorite ripple pattern, this afghan is alive with spectacular color. It will cast a warm glow over any room setting.

For how-to information, see Afghan Basics at the back of the book.

SIZE:
50″ × 72″

MATERIALS:
Worsted-weight, 4-ply yarn: two 4 oz. skeins Medium Brown; 3½ oz. each Rust, Brick, Bittersweet, Burnt Orange, Tangerine, Orange, Light Orange, Dark Yellow, Medium Yellow, Light Yellow, Pale Yellow, Medium Gray-Green. Crochet hook size J (6 mm), or size needed to obtain correct gauge.

GAUGE:
4 sc = 1″.

AFGHAN:
With Brown, ch 260 loosely.

Row 1: Sc in 3rd ch from hook, sc in each of next 5 ch, sc, ch 2, sc in next ch, sc in each of next 6 ch, * sk next 2 ch, sc in each of next 6 ch, sc, ch 2, sc in next ch, sc in each of next 6 ch, repeat from * across, end last repeat sc in each of next 5 ch, sk 1 ch, dc tightly in next ch—17 points. Unravel any extra chains. Ch 1, turn.

Row 2: Sc in first sc, sk next sc, sc in back lp of each of next 5 sc, sc in next ch, ch 2, sc in next ch, sc in back lp of each of next 6 sc, * sk next 2 sc, sc in back lp of each of next 6 sc, sc in next ch, ch 2, sc in next ch, sc in back lp of each of next 6 sc, repeat from * across, end last repeat sc in back lp of each of next 5 sc, sk next sc, dc in last sc. Ch 1, turn.

Rows 3 and 4: Repeat row 2. At end of row 4, finish last 2 lps of dc with Rust. Cut Brown. With Rust, ch 1, turn.

Row 5: With Rust, working over ends of Brown and Rust, repeat row 2.

Row 6: Repeat row 2, changing to Brick in last dc. With Brick, ch 1, turn.

Repeating row 2 for pattern and changing colors as before, work 2 rows Brick, 2 rows Bittersweet, 2 rows Burnt Orange, 2 rows Tangerine, 2 rows Orange, 2 rows Light Orange, 2 rows Dark Yellow, 2 rows Medium Yellow, 2 rows Light Yellow, 2 rows Pale Yellow, 2 rows Green, 4 rows Brown, 2 rows Rust. Repeat these 28 rows until you have 6 complete color stripes, end with 4 rows of Brown. End off.

GIRLS, BOYS, BABY'S TOYS

Afghans for babies and youngsters are always popular and fun to make. They are perfect as presents and are usually quick to work. Beginners can crochet the colorful Crayon Box, which is easily adjusted to either bed or rug size simply by adding a few extra crayons. A terrific pattern for boys and girls is Hats and Mittens, with real pompons and mitten strings sewn on. It would be hard to find a prettier set of nursery accessories than Candy-Stripe Ribbons and Bows, with a crib-sized afghan, matching pillow and bumper covers. Carrousel Horses will entertain Baby for many years, and, as an heirloom design, it should be passed on to the grandchildren. For a quick-and-easy carriage cover, either the Crocheted Coverlet or Baby Granny is a great choice—both are attractive and practical.

opposite page: *Candy-Stripe Ribbons and Bows*

CANDY-STRIPE RIBBONS AND BOWS

Ribbons and bows—what a delightful way to decorate a baby's room! New parents will appreciate this beautiful set of nursery accessories. For a special gift, customize trim and ribbon colors to match Baby's room.

For how-to information, see Afghan Basics at the back of the book.

BABY BLANKET

SIZE:

39" × 47"

MATERIALS:

Worsted-weight, 4-ply acrylic yarn: 14 oz. White, main color (MC); 7 oz. Pale Lilac (A); 3½ oz. each Medium Blue-Gray (B) and Spruce Green (C). Crochet hook size H (5 mm), or size required to obtain correct gauge. Tapestry needle. Sewing needle. Satin ribbon, ⅜" wide: 20 yd. White, 8 yd. Green, 6½ yd. Grape, 6 yd. Blue. White sewing thread. For backing: cotton fabric 45" wide, 1 yd.

GAUGE:

7 sts = 2", 6 rows = 2" (pat st).

BLANKET:

SOLID SQUARES (make 6): With MC, ch 42.

Row 1 (wrong side): Dc in 5th ch from hook and in each ch across—39 sts. Ch 1, turn.

Row 2: Sc in each dc across. Ch 2, turn.

Row 3: Skip first sc, dc in each sc across. Ch 1, turn. Repeat rows 2 and 3 eleven times, then work row 2 again, working 3 sc in last dc. Do not turn.

Continuing along left edge of square, work 3 sc along edge of next dc row, * sc in edge of next sc row, 2 sc along edge of next dc row, repeat from * eleven times. Working along foundation ch edge, work 3 sc in bottom of first dc, sc in each dc across to last dc, 3 sc in last dc. Work along remaining edge of square as on left edge, 3 sc in edge of next sc row, join with sl st to next sc—41 sc along each side plus 1 st in each corner. Fasten off. With A, work 1 row of sc around square, working 3 sc in each corner st—43 sc along each side plus 1 st in each corner.

MESH SQUARES (make 6): With MC, ch 44.

Row 1 (wrong side): Dc in 8th ch from hook, * ch 2, sk 2 ch, dc in next ch, repeat from * across. Ch 1, turn.

Row 2: Sc in each dc across and 2 sc in each ch-2 sp, end sc in turning ch. Ch 5, turn.

Row 3: Skip first 3 sc, dc in next sc, * ch 2, sk 2 sc, dc in next sc, repeat from * across. Repeat rows 2 and 3 eleven times. Work row 2 once more. Do not turn. With MC, work 1 row sc around edge of square as for solid square, being careful to have 41 sc along each side of square. With A, work 1 row sc around square as for solid square.

FINISHING:

Sew squares together having 3 across and 4 down, alternating solid and mesh squares.

EDGING: Row 1: Join C in any corner, ch 5, hdc in same st (first corner made) * ch 1, sk 1 sc, hdc in next sc, repeat from * across edge of first square, working last hdc in corner st of first square, sk corner st of next square, repeat from * across each edge of each square, working (hdc, ch 3, hdc) in corner st of last square on this side. Continue as established along each side of joined square, join with sl st to 3rd ch of starting ch-5—88 ch-2 sps along each long edge, 66 ch-2 sps along each short edge, ch-3 sp in each corner.

Rnd 2: In same corner, work sc, ch 3, sl st in first ch (picot made), sc, * (sc, picot, sc) in next ch-1 sp, sc in next ch-1 sp, repeat from * across, sc, picot, in ch-3 corner sp. Continue along each side in same manner. Join with sl st to first sc. Fasten off.

Rnd 3: With B, make a sl knot on hook, insert hook from back to front to back in sp between picot and ch-3 of rnd 1 in corner sp and complete sc; * ch 4, insert hook in sp below next picot and work sc in same manner, repeat from * around. Join with sl st to first sc.

Rnd 4: 5 sc in next ch-4 sp, sl st in next sc, repeat from * around. Fasten off.

Rnd 5: With A, make a sl knot on hook, insert hook from back to front to back around first sc of rnd 3 and complete sc; * ch 4, sc around next sc of rnd 3, repeat from * around. End sl st in first sc.

Rnd 6: * Ch 5, (2 dc, ch 3, 2 dc) in next sc, ch 5, sc in next sc, repeat from * around. End sl st in first st.

Rnd 7: * Sc in next ch-5 sp, (ch 1, dc) five times in next ch-3 sp, ch 1, sc in next ch-5 sp, ch 1, repeat from * around. Join with sl st to first st.

Rnd 8: * (Sc in next ch-1 sp, picot) five times, sc in next ch-1 sp, repeat from * around. Sl st in first sc. Fasten off.

RIBBON TRIMMING: For each mesh square, cut lengths of ribbon as follows: Blue, two pieces each 5″ and 12″; Green, two pieces each 8″ and 14″; White, two pieces each 6½″, 9″, 11″, 13″ and 16″; Grape, two 10″ pieces and one 17″ piece. Weave ribbons diagonally, alternating colored ribbons with White ribbons. Make 2 small ribbon bows each with Blue, Green, and Grape. Sew one bow in center of each solid square.

LINING: Cut squares of white fabric same size as mesh squares, adding ¼″ seam allowance all around. Turn seam allowance under and press. Sew lining to back of mesh squares.

CRIB BUMPER COVERS

SIZE:
Two covers 49″ × 10″; two covers 27½″ × 10″

MATERIALS:
Worsted-weight, 4-ply acrylic yarn: 17½ oz. White (MC); 3½ oz. each Pale Lilac (A), Medium Blue-Gray (B), and Spruce Green (C). Crochet hook size H (5 mm), or size required to obtain correct gauge. Sewing needle. Satin ribbon, ⅜″ wide: 2 yd. each Green, Grape, and Blue. White sewing thread. For backing, cotton fabric 45″ wide, 1½ yd. Standard-size crib bumpers.

GAUGE:
7 sts = 2″; 6 rows = 2″ (pat st).

BUMPER COVERS:
LONG PIECE (make 2): With MC, ch 173, Work even in pat st as for solid square of blanket on 172 sts for 26 rows. Work 1 row of sc around entire piece, working 3 sc in each corner. Fasten off.

SHORT PIECE (make 2): With MC, ch 99. Work even in pat st as for solid square of blanket on 96 sts for 26 rows. Work 1 row of sc around entire piece, working 3 sc in each corner. Fasten off.

FINISHING:
With A, work 1 row of sc along top edge only of each piece. Fasten off. Work rows 1–4 of blanket edging along top edge only.

BACKING: Cut material same size as each crocheted piece, allowing ¼″ all around for hem. Turn hem under and sew in place. Sew top edge only of each crocheted piece to matching fabric piece.

TIES: With MC, make thirty-two 8″ long chains. Sew 1 chain to top and bottom corners of each crocheted and fabric piece.

BOWS: Make 8 bows in each of 3 ribbon colors. Sew 1 ribbon of each color in diagonal arrangement centered on each short crocheted piece, and 3 sets of 3 ribbons each spaced along each long crocheted piece. Place bumper covers over crib bumpers.

PILLOW

SIZE:
15″ × 15″, including edging

MATERIALS:
Worsted-weight, 4-ply acrylic yarn: 3½ oz. each White (MC), Pale Lilac (A), Medium Blue-Gray (B), and Spruce Green (C). Crochet hook size H (5 mm), or size required to obtain correct gauge. Sewing needle. Satin ribbon, ⅜″ wide: 3½ yd. White, 1⅓ yd. Green, 1⅙ yd. Grape, 1 yd. Blue. White sewing thread. Piece of white cotton fabric, 22½″ long × 11½″ wide. Stuffing. Pillow form, 11″ square.

GAUGE:
7 sts = 2″, 6 rows = 2″ (pat st).

PILLOW:
Make 1 mesh square, same as for blanket. Work edging and ribbon trimming in same manner. Cover 11″-square pillow form with white material and sew the crocheted piece to pillow, leaving edging free.

HATS AND MITTENS

This whimsical, child-size afghan has hats and mittens crocheted right in—and it's reversible, too! For added fun, three-dimensional pompons, hat rims, and mitten strings are attached to one side of the afghan.

For how-to information, see Afghan Basics at the back of the book.

SIZE:
44″ × 50″

MATERIALS:
Worsted-weight, 4-ply acrylic yarn: 30 oz. Blue (B); 15 oz. White (W). Crochet hook size F (3.75 mm), or size required to obtain correct gauge.

GAUGE:
4 hdc = 1″; 13 rows = 5″.

AFGHAN:

Notes: Afghan is made in 3 panels, all worked in hdc. Designs are crocheted in. Always carry unused color along inside of work: that is, when working White sts, work over Blue strand; when working Blue sts, work over White strand. At end of row and just before changing colors within the row, pull the carried strand to prevent having a loop of yarn showing through work. When changing colors, finish last hdc of one color by drawing new color through 3 loops on hook.

CENTER PANEL: With W, ch 54.

Row 1: Working over B strand, with W, hdc in 3rd ch from hook and in each ch across—52 hdc. Ch 2, turn each row.

Row 2: Working over B strand, with W, hdc in each hdc across.

Rows 3 and 4: 2 W, 48 B, 2 W.

Row 5: 2 W, 2 B, 44 W, 2 B, 2 W.

Row 6 (Basic row): 2 W, 2 B, 1 W, 42 B, 1 W, 2 B, 2 W.

Rows 7–12: Repeat row 6.

Row 13: 2 W, 2 B, 1 W, 7 B; following Chart 1 for hat, work 28 W; 7 B, 1 W, 2 B, 2 W.

Rows 14–32: Continue to work basic row for sides of panel, following chart for center 28 sts.

Rows 33–48: Repeat row 6.

Row 49: 2 W, 2 B, 1 W, 4 B; following chart 2 for mittens, work 27 B, 6 W, 1 B, 4 B, 1 W, 2 B, 2 W.

Rows 50–65: Continue to work basic row for sides of panel, following chart for center 34 sts.

Rows 66–88: Repeat row 6.

Rows 89–108: Repeat rows 13–32.

Rows 109–116: Repeat row 6.

Row 117: Repeat row 5.

Rows 118 and 119: Repeat row 3.

Rows 120 and 121: Repeat row 2.
End off.

SIDE PANEL (make 2): Work as for center panel through row 12.

Rows 13–29: Work as for rows 49–65 of center panel.

Rows 30–52: Repeat row 6.

Rows 53–72: Work as for rows 13–32 of center panel.

Rows 73–88: Repeat row 6.

Rows 89–105: Repeat rows 13–29.

Rows 106–116: Repeat row 6.

Row 117: Repeat row 5.

Rows 118 and 119: Repeat row 3.

Rows 120 and 121: Repeat row 2.
End off.

FINISHING:

HAT RIM (make 2 for each hat): With White, ch 8. Hdc in 3rd ch from hook and in each ch across—6 hdc.

Work even in hdc, working in back loops only, for 16 rows. End off. Sew in place at bottom of hat on each side of afghan.

Make 3 white pompons. Sew to top of each hat on one side of afghan only.

Crochet a white chain about 24″ long for each pair of mittens. Sew to afghan with invisible stitches to join mittens.

Sew or crochet panels together.

BORDER:

With Blue, work 4 rows of sc around afghan, work sc, ch 2, sc in each corner each rnd. Join each rnd.

Last Rnd: * Ch 3, sl st in first ch, sk 2 sc on border, sc in next sc, repeat from * around. Join; end off.

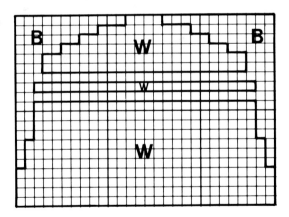

CHART 1

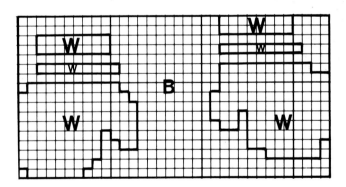

CHART 2

CARROUSEL HORSES

Brightly colored carrousel horses gallop across this lively afghan. The perfect size for a child's coverlet, it is certain to add fun and enchantment to a youngster's room.

For how-to information, see Afghan Basics at the back of the book.

SIZE:
40″ × 50″

MATERIALS:
Worsted-weight, 4-ply acrylic yarn: 21 oz. White; 3½ oz. each Light Powder-Blue (A), Medium Powder-Blue (B), Goldenrod (C), Dark Goldenrod (D), Light Strawberry Pink (E), Fuchsia (F), Light Blue-Green (G), Spruce Green (H), and Pale Lilac (I). Afghan hook size H (5 mm), or size required to obtain correct gauge. Crochet hook size H (5 mm). Tapestry needle.

GAUGE:
16 sts = 4″; 15 rows = 4″.

AFGHAN STITCH:
Ch desired number of sts.

Row 1: Keeping all lps on hook, pull up a lp in 2nd ch from hook and in each ch across.

To Work Lps Off: Yo hook, pull through first lp, * yo hook, pull through next 2 lps, repeat from * across until 1 lp remains. Lp that remains on hook always counts as first st of next row.

Row 2: Keeping all lps on hook, pull up a lp under 2nd vertical bar and under each vertical bar across. Work lps off as before.

AFGHAN:
With White and afghan hook, ch 152.

Work row 1 and row 2 of afghan stitch. Repeat row 2 until there are 176 rows. Sl st in each vertical bar across. End off.

EMBROIDERY:
Mark 29th st in from lower right-hand corner on first row of afghan. Beginning on this st, following chart, embroider design in cross-stitch. Embroider large dots in French knots, using E on bridle, H on saddle for horse at right; A on horse at bottom center; C on horse at left. Embroider heavy lines in outline stitch: B on bow at bottom right, D on horse above, C on bow above; F on horse at bottom center, H for his eye and for bow above, B on horse above. Work 5 long E sts to form star; G for bow at left, H for legs and features of horse above, I for saddle, F for bow above.

FINISHING:
With G and crochet hook, work 1 rnd sc around afghan, working 1 sc in each st at top and bottom of afghan, 1 sc in each row on sides and 3 sc in each corner. Sl st in first sc. Ch 1. Work 2 more rnds of sc, working 3 sc in each corner sc. Join each rnd. Ch 1.

Last Rnd: * Sc in 4 sc, (sc, ch 3, sc) in next sc, repeat from * around, spacing pat so as to have ch-3 picot in each corner. Join; end off.

CARROUSEL AFGHAN CHART

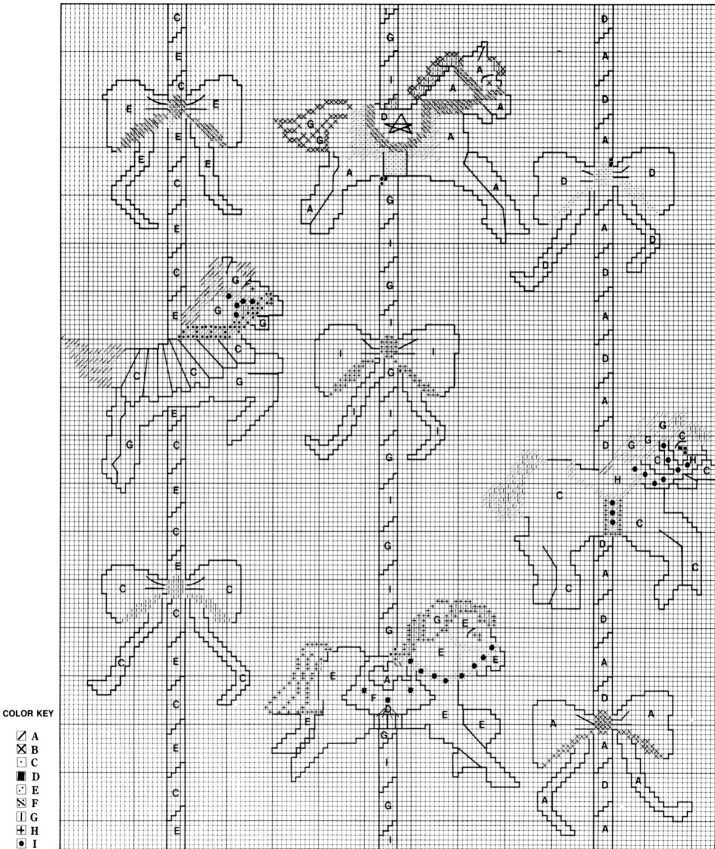

COLOR KEY

- ◿ A
- ☒ B
- ⊡ C
- ■ D
- ⊡ E
- ◩ F
- ▯ G
- ✚ H
- ⦿ I

QUICK-CROCHET CARRIAGE COVER

This delightful coverlet for a baby's carriage is easy to crochet and quick to work. It is an ideal pattern for a last-minute gift.

For how-to information, see Afghan Basics at the back of the book.

SIZE:
26" × 38"

MATERIALS:
Fingering yarn: 10½ oz. Pink; 3½ oz. White. Crochet hook size K (7 mm), or size required to obtain correct gauge.

GAUGE:
3 hdc = 1" (worked with double strand of yarn).

AFGHAN:
Entire afghan is worked with double strand of yarn.

COVER STRIPS (make 5): With double strand of Pink, ch 11.

Row 1: Hdc in 3rd ch from hook (counts as 2 hdc) and in each ch across—10 hdc. Ch 2, turn.

Row 2: Hdc in back lp of 2nd hdc and in back lp of each hdc across, hdc in top of turning ch. Ch 2, turn. Repeat row 2 fifty-nine times (61 rows from start). End off.

LOOP EDGING: With double strand of White, working on long side of first strip, sc in edge of first row, * ch 4, sk next row, sc in edge of next row, repeat from * across—30 lps. End off.

JOINING ROW: With double strand White, working on long side of 2nd strip, sc in edge of first row, ch 2, sc in first ch-4 lp of first strip, * ch 2, sk next row on 2nd strip, sc in edge of next row on 2nd strip, ch 2, sc in next ch-4 lp on first strip, repeat from * across. End off. Join all strips in this way.

OUTER LOOP EDGING: With double strand White, sc in first hdc at top of first strip, * (ch 4, sk next 2 hdc, sc in next hdc) three times, ch 4, sc in sc between ch-4 lps, ch 4, sc in first hdc of next strip, repeat from * across upper edge; working along long side of strip, ch 4, sk first row, sc in next row, ch 4, sk next row, sc in next row, continue in this way around entire outer edge of cover. Join with a sl st in first sc. End off.

OUTER STRIP: With double strand of Pink, ch 14. Work same as for first strip on 13 hdc for 253 rows. Piece should measure 135". Weave first row to last row, forming circle.

With double strand of White, join outer strip to outer loop edging, same as 2nd strip was joined to first strip, working corners as follows: Ch 2, insert hook through 6 ridges on outer strip, yo hook, draw lp through, yo hook and through 2 lps on hook, ch 2, sc in next ch-4 lp on blanket. Continue this way around. End off. Steam lightly.

BABY GRANNY

For a lovely carriage cover, try this traditional granny-square pattern using an unusual color combination of aqua, yellow, and pink. Finish with a fringe made of crocheted chains.

For how-to information, see Afghan Basics at the back of the book.

SIZE:
36″ × 36″, plus fringe

MATERIALS:
Sport-weight acrylic yarn: 10 oz. Aqua; 4 oz. each Yellow and Light Pink. Crochet hook size F (3.75 mm), or size required to obtain correct gauge. Tapestry needle.

GAUGE:
Each square = 3¼″.

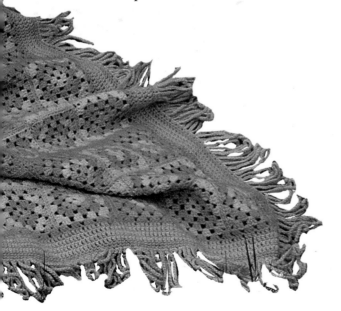

Quick-Crochet Carriage Cover (left);
Baby Granny (right).

BLANKET:

SQUARE 1 (make 33): With Aqua, ch 6. Sl st in first ch to form ring.

Rnd 1: Ch 3 (counts as 1 dc), 2 dc in ring, (ch 2, 3 dc in ring), three times, ch 2, sl st in top of ch 3 at beg of rnd. End off.

Rnd 2: Join Yellow with a sl st in a ch-2 sp; ch 3, 2 dc in same sp, ch 2, 3 dc in same sp, (ch 1, 3 dc, ch 2, 3 dc in next sp) three times, ch 1, join with a sl st to top of ch 3. End off.

Rnd 3 Join Pink with a sl st in corner ch-2 sp, ch 3, 2 dc in same sp, ch 2, 3 dc in same sp, (ch 1, 3 dc in next sp, ch 1, 3 dc, ch 2, 3 dc in next corner sp) three times, ch 1, 3 dc in next sp, ch 1, join with a sl st to top of ch 3. End off.

Rnd 4: Join aqua with a sl st in corner ch-2 sp; ch 3, 2 dc in same sp; ch 2, 3 dc in same sp, * (ch 1, 3 dc in next sp) twice, ch 1, 3 dc, ch 2, 3 dc in corner sp, repeat from * twice, ch 1, (3 dc in next sp, ch 1) twice, join with a sl st to top of ch 3. End off.

SQUARE 2 (make 30): With Yellow, work as for square 1 through rnd 1.

Rnd 2 With Aqua, work as for square 1.

Rnd 3: With Pink, work as for square 1.

Rnd 4: With Yellow, work as for square 1.

SQUARE 3 (make 10): With Yellow, work as for square 1 through rnd 1.

Rnd 2: With Pink, work as for square 1.

Rnd 3: With Aqua, work as for square 1.

Rnd 4: With Yellow, work as for square 1.

SQUARE 4 (make 8): With Aqua, work as for square 1 through rnd 1.

Rnd 2: With Pink, work as for square 1.

Rnd 3: With Yellow, work as for square 1.

Rnd 4: With Aqua, work as for square 1.

JOINING SQUARES: LARGE SQUARE 1 (make 5): Following chart 1, arrange 9 squares into one square, 3 squares by 3 squares. With any matching color, sew squares tog, picking up back lp of each st around edge of square.

LARGE SQUARE 2 (make 4): Following chart 2, join squares same as for large square 1.

LARGE SQUARE EDGING: Join Pink with a sl st in corner ch-2 sp of any large square, ch 3, 2 dc in same sp, ch 2, 3 dc in same sp, * (ch 1, 3 dc in next ch-1 sp) three times, ch 1, 3 dc in corner ch-2 sp, ch 1, 3 dc in corner ch-2 sp of next square, repeat from * once, (ch 1, 3 dc in next ch-1 sp) three times, ch 1, 3 dc, ch 2, 3 dc in corner ch-2 sp, repeat from

first * around, end last repeat sl st to top of starting ch 3. End off. Work same edging around all 9 large squares.

JOINING LARGE SQUARES: Following chart 3, join 9 large squares into one square, 3 squares by 3 squares. With Pink, sew squares tog, picking up back lp of each st around edge of each square.

OUTER EDGING: Join Aqua in any dc (not in corner), ch 3, dc in next dc and in each dc around, working 3 dc, ch 2, 3 dc in each corner. Join with a sl st to top of ch 3; do not turn.

Rnd 2: Ch 3, dc in each dc around, working 2 dc, ch 2, 2 dc in each corner ch-2 sp, join with a sl st to top of ch 3.

Rnds 3 and 4: Repeat rnd 2. Drop Aqua at end of rnd 4.

Rnd 5: With Pink, sc in each st around, working 2 sc, ch 2, 2 sc in each corner ch-2 sp. Join with a sl st in first sc. End off.

Rnd 6: Pick up Aqua, repeat rnd 5. Join; end off.

FINISHING:

Press blanket on wrong side with damp cloth and cool iron. Dry thoroughly.

FRINGE: Join Aqua in any sc, ch 40, sl st in same st as joining, * sc in next sc, sl st in next sc, ch 40, sl st in same sc, repeat from * around. Join with a sl st in first st. End off. Weave in all yarn ends.

CHART 1		
1	2	1
3	1	3
1	2	1

CHART 2		
2	1	2
4	2	4
2	1	2

CHART 3		
1	2	1
2	1	2
1	2	1

BABY ROSE

Create this lovely eyelet crochet, complete with all the added frills you could wish for. It is laced with satin ribbon and has sewn-on roses, bows, and an eyelet ruffle.

For how-to information, see Afghan Basics at the back of the book.

SIZE:
42″ square

MATERIALS:
Sport-weight, cotton yarn, 28 oz. White. Crochet hook size H (5 mm), or size required to obtain correct gauge. Satin ribbon, ⅜″ wide, 14 yd. Dark Pink, 5 yd. Light Pink. 35 small Light Pink satin bows. 24 appliqué roses. White eyelet, 5 yd. Tapestry needle.

GAUGE:
14 dc = 4″; 8 rows = 4″; 3-dc groups = 5″; 2 picots = 5″.

AFGHAN:
Note: Afghan is made in one piece. Ch 139. Sc in 2nd ch from hook and in each ch across—138 sc. Turn.

Row 1: Ch 3 (always counts as first dc), dc in 2nd sc from hook (edge sts), * dc in 16 sc, ch 1, sk 1 sc for vertical beading column, dc in next sc, ch 1, sk 2 sc, 5 dc in next sc, (ch 1, sk 4 sc, 5 dc in next sc) twice, sk 1 sc, dc in next sc, ch 1, sk 1 sc, repeat from * across, end dc in last 2 sc (edge sts).

Row 2: Ch 3, dc in 2nd dc from hook, ch 5, ** sc in center dc of 5-dc group, * ch 2, (dc, ch 3, sl st in top of dc first worked—picot made), dc in ch-1 sp, ch 2, sc in

center dc of 5-dc group, repeat from * once, ch 1, dc in next dc, ch 1, dc in 16 dc, ch 1, dc in next dc, ch 2, repeat from ** across, end dc in next dc, dc in top of ch-3.

Row 3: Ch 3, dc in 2nd dc, * dc in 16 dc, ch 1, dc in next dc, (5 dc in next sc, ch 1) twice, 5 dc in next sc, dc in next dc, ch 1, repeat from * across, end last repeat ch 1, dc in next dc, dc in top of ch-3. Repeat rows 2 and 3 four times. Ch 1, turn.

*** Next Row: Sc in first 2 sts, sc across, working 17 sc along each pat block, sc in each ch-1 sp and 16 sc across each 16-dc block, end sc in last dc, sc in top of ch-3. Ch 3, turn.

HORIZONTAL BEADING ROW: Dc in 2nd sc, * ch 1, sk 1 sc, dc in next sc, repeat from * across, end dc in last sc. Ch 1, turn.

Row 2: Sc in each dc and ch-1 sp, working 16 sc over each 16-dc block and 16 dc over each pat block, end sc in last dc, sc in top of ch-3. Ch 3, turn. *******

Row 3: Dc in 2nd sc, ch 1, sk 2 sc, 5 dc in next sc, (ch 1, sk 4 sc, 5 dc in next sc) twice, sk 2 sc, dc in next sc, * ch 1, sk 1 sc (beading), dc in 16 sc, ch 1, sk 1 sc, dc in next sc, ch 1, sk 1 sc, 5 dc in next sc, (ch 1, sk 4 sc, 5 dc in next sc) twice, sk 2 sc, dc in next sc, repeat from * across, end ch 1, sk 1 sc, dc in next 16 sc, dc in last 2 sc. Ch 3, turn.

Row 4: Dc in 2nd dc, ** dc in 16 dc, ch 1, dc in next dc, * ch 2, sc in center dc of 5-dc group, ch 2, (dc, picot, dc) in ch-1 sp, repeat from * once, ch 2, sc in center dc of 5-dc group, ch 1, dc in last dc, ch 1, repeat from ** across, end last repeat sc in center of dc of 5-dc group, ch 3, dc in last dc, dc in top of ch-3. Ch 3, turn.

Row 5: Dc in 2nd dc, * (5 dc in next sc, ch 1) twice, 5 dc in next sc, dc in next dc, ch 1, dc in 16 dc, ch 1, dc in next dc, repeat from * across, end dc in top of ch-3. Ch 3, turn.

Repeat rows 4 and 5 four times. Repeat the 3 rows from *** to ***, working 17 sc over the 16-dc blocks and 16 sc over the pat blocks. Repeat from row 1 until there are 6 rows of blocks (5 horizontal beading rows). Sc along top edge, ch 1, working (sc, ch 1, sc) in each corner. Continue working 2 rnds sc around afghan, join with sl st in ch-1 sp.

Next Rnd: Ch 3 (counts as first dc), dc in each sc around, working 5 dc in each corner sp. End off.

FINISHING:

Dampen afghan and block to 40″ square. Sew a rose appliqué to center of each dc block. Weave Dark Pink ribbon through vertical beading rows, then through horizontal beading rows. Sew a bow to each intersection of beading rows to define squares. Measure eyelet plus 3″ for each side. Weave Light Pink ribbon through beading row on eyelet. Turn 1½″ at each end of eyelet to inside. Pin to edges and sew in place.

Baby Rose (left); *Baby Quilt and Pillow* (right).

BABY QUILT AND PILLOW

Charming nursery playmates in filet crochet are easy enough for beginners to tackle yet are unusually elegant. Use decoratively on Baby's coverlet and choose a favorite for a matching pillow motif.

For how-to information, see Afghan Basics at the back of the book.

SIZES:
Quilt, 29½" × 29½", plus 2¼" ruffle all around; pillow, 11" square

MATERIALS:
Mercerized crochet cotton, No. 8, three 300-yd. balls Pink. Steel crochet hook No. 7 (1.65 mm), or size required to obtain correct gauge. Cotton fabric, 2 yd. Batting. Pillow form, 11" square. Double-faced satin ribbon, ¼" wide, 6 yd.

GAUGE:
Each motif = 8½" × 8½".

PATTERN STITCH:
Motifs are worked in filet crochet. One block (bl) is 4 dc, each additional bl is 3 dc more. One space (sp) is dc, ch 2, dc; each additional sp is ch 2, dc. Follow charts from right to left on right-side rows, from left to right on wrong-side rows.

AFGHAN:
PATTERN SQUARES (make 2 of each motif): Ch 77.

Row 1 (right side): Dc in 8th ch from hook, * ch 2, sk 2 ch, dc in next ch, repeat from * across—24 sps.

Ch 5 (counts as dc, ch 2) to turn each row; work last dc of each row in 3rd ch of ch-5. Continue as established, working rows 2 to 33 from charts. Do not turn at end of last row.

EDGING: Ch 1, work 1 rnd sc evenly around 4 sides, working 2 sc in each corner. End off.

FINISHING:

COVERLET: Cut coverlet front, 29½" × 29½". Cut back same size. Cut fabric strip 5½" wide × 200" long, piecing together as necessary for ruffle. Stitch ruffle ends together; press seams open. Fold ruffle in half lengthwise, right-side-out; press. Using a long basting stitch, gather ruffle ½" from raw edges to fit around coverlet front. Stitch ruffle to right side of coverlet front. Stitch coverlet front and back together, right sides facing, making ½" seams and leaving an opening in one side for turning. Turn coverlet to right side. Insert batting in raw edges and slip-stitch opening closed. Sew squares to top of coverlet, with 1 in each corner and 1 in center. Sew a bow to corner of each square.

PILLOW: Cut one 12″-square pillow front from fabric. Cut pillow back same size. Cut a strip of fabric 5½″ wide × 55″ long for ruffle, piece together as necessary. Stitch ruffle ends together; press seam open. Fold ruffle in half lengthwise, right-side-out; press. Using a long basting stitch, gather ruffle ½″ from raw edges to fit around pillow front. Stitch pillow front and back together with ruffle in between making ½″ seams and leaving an opening in one side for turning. Turn pillow to right side. Insert pillow form. Turn in raw edges and slip-stitch opening closed. Sew crocheted square to pillow front. Tie a bow in center.

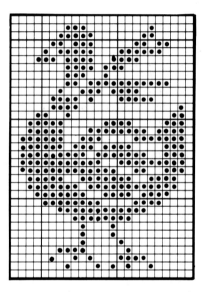

SWEET DREAMS

Tuck Baby in surrounded by a toy chest of nursery favorites. Blanket is crocheted in afghan stitch, with the toys embroidered in cross-stitch later. Cross-stitch your favorite friend on a matching pillow.

For how-to information, see Afghan Basics at the back of the book.

SIZES:
Blanket: 46″ × 54″
Pillow: 15″ square

MATERIALS:
Worsted-weight, 4-ply yarn: 42 oz. Off-white (A); 7 oz. each Light Blue (B) and Light Pink (C); 3½ oz. each Medium Blue (D), Cream (E), and Camel (F); small amount Brown (G). Afghan hook size J (6 mm), or size required to obtain correct gauge. Crochet hook size J. Tapestry needle. Pillow form, 15″ square. Fabric, ½ yd.

GAUGE:
14 sts = 4″; 12 rows = 4″.

AFGHAN STITCH:
Make a ch the required number of sts.

Row 1: Draw up a lp in 2nd ch from hook and in each ch across.

To Work Lps Off: Yo and pull through 1 lp, * yo and pull through 2 lps, repeat from * across. Lp that remains on hook counts as first st of next row.

Row 2: Draw up a lp in 2nd vertical bar and in each vertical bar across. Work lps off as before. Repeat row 2 for afghan st.

Finishing Row: * Pull up a lp under vertical bar and through the lp on hook, repeat from * across. End off.

BLANKET:
Note: To change color, work st to the point where there are 3 lps on hook, yo and finish st with new color. Do not carry colors across back of work. Use a separate ball of yarn for each color section. Cut and join colors as necessary.

With afghan hook and A, ch 162.

Row 1: Work in afghan st.

Row 2: Draw up a lp in 2nd vertical bar, * bring yarn forward, with left thumb, hold yarn below next vertical bar, draw up a lp through this vertical bar—purl st made, draw up a lp in next vertical bar, repeat from * across to last 2 vertical bars, purl st in next vertical bar, insert hook in last vertical bar and the st directly behind it and draw up a lp. Work lps off each row.

Row 3: Purl st in 2nd vertical bar, * draw up a lp in next vertical bar, purl st in next vertical bar, repeat from * across to last 2 vertical bars, draw up a lp in next vertical bar, draw up a lp in last vertical bar as before. Repeat rows 2 and 3 for pat st.

Rows 4–28: Continue in pat st for 16 more rows A, 2 rows B, 2 rows A, 2 rows C, 2 rows A, 2 rows B.

Rows 29–46: With A, pat st on 36 sts, place marker on hook, afghan st on next 30 sts, place marker, pat st on next 30 sts, place marker, afghan st on next 30 sts, place marker, pat st on next 36 sts. Carry markers each row.

Rows 47 and 48: With C, pat st on 36 sts; with A, afghan st on next 30 sts, pat st on next 30 sts, afghan st on next 30 sts, with C, pat st on next 36 sts. Work lps off in colors as they appear.

Rows 49–62: Repeat row 47, working 2 rows A only, 2 rows B instead of C, 2 rows A only, 2 rows C, 6 rows A only. Drop markers.

Rows 63–74: With A, pat st on 66 sts, place marker on hook, afghan st on next 30 sts, place marker, pat st on next 66 sts.

Rows 75 and 76: With B, pat st on 66 sts; with A, afghan st on 30 sts; with B, pat st on 66 sts.

Rows 77 and 78: Repeat row 63.

Rows 79 and 80: With C instead of B, repeat row 75.

Rows 81 and 82: Repeat row 63.

Rows 83 and 84: Repeat row 75.

Rows 85–96: Repeat row 63.

Rows 97–102: Repeat row 29.

Rows 103 and 104: Repeat row 47.

Rows 105 and 106: Repeat row 29.

Rows 107 and 108: With B instead of C, repeat row 47.

Rows 109 and 110: Repeat row 29.

Rows 111 and 112: Repeat row 47.

Rows 113–130: Repeat row 29.

Rows 131–158: Continue in pat st on all sts, working 2 rows B, 2 rows A, 2 rows C, 2 rows A, 2 rows B, 18 rows A. Work finishing row. End off.

EDGING: Rnd 1: From right side, with crochet hook, and C, sc evenly around blanket, working 3 sc in each corner.

Rnd 2: With A, ch 1, sc through back lp of each sc around.

Rnd 3: With B, repeat rnd 2. End off.

EMBROIDERY: Embroider a motif in cross st in each afghan stitch square as shown in photograph, following charts.

PILLOWTOP:

With A, ch 46. **Rows 1–6:** Work in pat st same as blanket.

Rows 7–40: Pat st on 8 sts, place marker on hook, afghan st on next 30 sts, place marker, pat st on next 8 sts.

Rows 42–46: Repeat rows 1–6. work finishing row. End off.

EDGING: Work same as blanket.

EMBROIDERY: Embroider any motif in cross-stitch following charts.

TO MAKE PILLOW: Cut out pillow front from fabric, 16″ square. Cut pillow back same size. With right sides together, stitch pillow front and back together, making ½″ seams and leaving an opening in one side for turning. Turn pillow to right side. Insert pillow form. Turn in raw edges and slip-stitch opening closed.

Sew pillowtop to front of pillow.

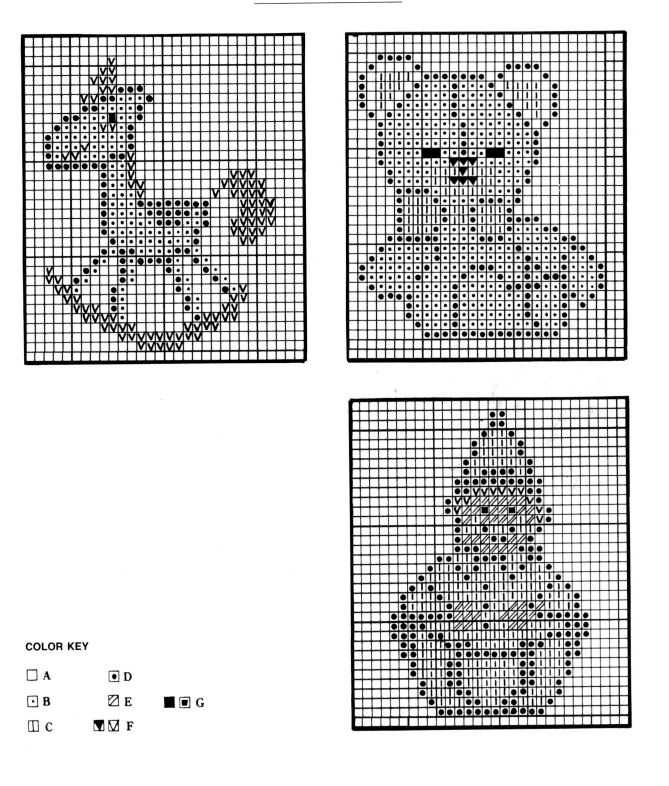

COLOR KEY

☐ A   ⊡ D

⊡ B   ▨ E   ■ ▣ G

⫿ C   ▼▽ F

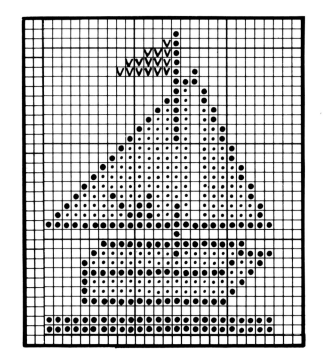

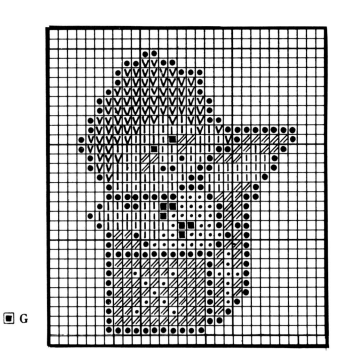

COLOR KEY

A

B

C

D

E

F

G

CRAYON BOX

Beginners can make this vibrant child's afghan using quick-to-master single crochet. The overall size can easily be enlarged or reduced simply by adding or omitting "crayons."

For how-to information, see Afghan Basics at the back of the book.

SIZE:
52" × 72"

MATERIALS:
Worsted-weight, 4-ply yarn, 3½ oz. 12 colors (choose one light and one dark tone of 6 colors), 14 oz. Black. Crochet hooks sizes H (5 mm) and I (5.5 mm). Tapestry needle.

GAUGE:
7 sc = 2".

AFGHAN:

CRAYON: Beg at tip, with dark color and I hook, ch 3.

Row 1: Sc in 2nd ch from hook and in last ch. Ch 1, turn each row.

Row 2: 2 sc in first sc, sc in last sc.

Row 3: 2 sc in first sc, sc in 2 sc.

Rows 4–17: 2 sc in first sc, sc in each sc across—18 sc.

Rows 18–20: Sc in each sc. Cut dark color; attach light color.

Rows 21–76: Work even with light color for 56 rows. Cut light color; attach dark color.

Rows 77–82: Work even with dark color for 6 rows. End off.

Make one more crayon in the same manner. Make two crayons with reverse colors. Repeat with all colors—25 crayons.

TRIANGLE (make 22): With Black and H hook, ch 2.

Row 1: Sc in 2nd ch from hook. Ch 1, turn each row.

Row 2: 2 sc in sc.

Row 3: 2 sc in first sc, sc in last sc. Continue to inc 1 sc each row until there are 18 sc. End off.

HALF-TRIANGLE FOR CORNER (make 4): With Black and H hook, ch 2.

Row 1: Sc in 2nd ch from hook. Ch 1, turn each row.

Row 2: Sc in sc.

Row 3: 2 sc in sc.

Row 4: Sc in 2 sc.

Row 5: 2 sc in first sc, sc in last sc.

Row 6: Sc in 3 sc.

Row 7: 2 sc in first sc, sc in 2 sc.

Row 8: Sc in 4 sc. Continue to inc 1 sc every other row until there are 9 sc. End off.

CRAYON EDGINGS: From right side, with Black and size I hook, beg in corner of last row of crayon, sc in end of row, * ch 1, sk 1 row, sc in end of next row, repeat from * along side of crayon to beg of point—34 sc. End off. Attach Black to opposite side of crayon on same row, work same sc, ch 1 edging along 2nd side of crayon to last row. End off. Work same edgings on all crayons.

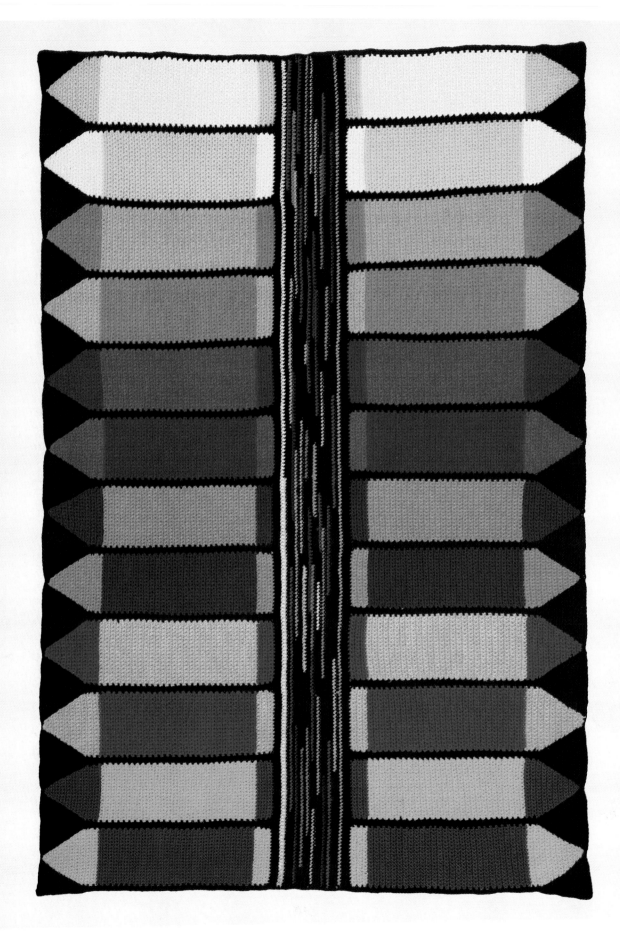

ASSEMBLE CRAYONS: Place right sides of 2 crayons tog. With Black in tapestry needle, sew 2 crayons tog, overcasting through back lps only of sc's and chs. Sew 12 crayons tog chromatically in this way; repeat for other side of afghan.

Sew triangles and corner in place.

CENTER PANEL: With Black and I hook, work 3 rows sc across ends of 12 crayons. End off. Work same 3 rows sc across 2nd side. Join a light color and work 1 row sc, changing to another color if yarn is running out. Work in rows of sc for 6″ or until yarn is used up, changing from Black to a color for a "scribbling" effect.

Sew or crochet 2 halves of afghan tog. With Black, work 1 or 2 rows of sc around afghan, working 3 sc in each corner. Join; end off.

WARM AND WINTRY

Here is a superb collection of afghans designed to bring warmth and cheer as the days grow shorter and colder. Some celebrate the magic of winter with scenes of skaters and skiers and fresh-fallen snow. Others will enhance your Christmases year after year with holiday patterns that are beautiful and lasting. Knitters will enjoy Winter Wonderland, a coverlet made extra-warm by the two layers created by double knitting. Certain to warm your toes and brighten any setting is Snowfire, a portable crochet project with lacy-white snowflakes framed in flame-red yarn. And to add to the Yuletide festivities, create a welcoming ring of poinsettias, or a spirited fisherman Aran decorated with sprigs of holly.

opposite page: *Holly Aran*

HOLLY ARAN

A spirited adaptation of Aran knitting, this graceful afghan will "deck your halls" with holiday cheer. The holly leaves are knit from a chart; the holly berries are French knots added later.

For how-to information, see Afghan Basics at the back of the book.

SIZE:
48" × 50"

MATERIALS:
Worsted-weight, 4-ply yarn: 35 oz. Off-white (A); 3½ oz. each Green (B) and Red (C). Circular knitting needles, 29" long, No. 6 and 8 (4.25 and 5 mm), or size required to obtain correct gauge. Double-pointed needle. Tapestry needle.

GAUGE:
20 sts = 4"; 28 rows = 4".

SPECIAL ABBREVIATIONS:
LC: Left Cross: Sl 2 sts to dp needle and hold in front of work, p 1, k 2 from dp needle.

RC: Right Cross: Sl st to dp needle and hold in back of work, k 2, p 1 from dp needle.

PATTERN STITCHES:
PATTERN 1:
Rows 1, 3, and 4: Knit.
Row 2: Purl. Repeat rows 1–4 for pat 1.

PATTERN 2 (worked on 10 sts):
Rows 1, 3, and 7: P 2, k 6, p 2.
Row 2 and All Wrong-Side Rows: K 2, p 6, k 2.

Row 5: P 2, sl 3 sts to dp needle and hold in front of work, k 3, k 3 from dp needle, p 2.
Row 8: Repeat row 2. Repeat rows 1–8 for pat 2.

PATTERN 3 (worked on 20 sts):
Row 1: P 2, k 2, (k 1, p 1) six times, k 2, p 2.
Row 2 and All Wrong-Side Rows: K the k sts, p the p sts.
Row 3: P 2, LC, (k 1, p 1) five times, RC, p 2.
Row 5: P 3, LC, (k 1, p 1) four times, RC, p 3.
Row 7: P 4, LC, (k 1, p 1) three times, RC, p 4.
Row 9: P 5, LC, (k 1, p 1) twice, RC, p 5.
Row 11: P 6, LC, k 1, p 1, RC, p 6.
Row 13: P 7, LC, RC, p 7.
Row 15: P 8 sl 2 sts to dp needle and hold in front of work, k 2, k 2 from dp needle, p 8.
Row 17: P 7, RC, LC, p 7.
Row 19: P 20.
Row 20: K 20. Repeat rows 1–20 for pat 3.

PATTERN 4 (worked on 20 sts):
Note: On pat 4 RC's, k st from dp needle instead of p.
Rows 1–16: Work same as rows 1–16 for pat 3.
Row 17: P 7, RC, LC, p 7.

148

Row 19: P 6, RC, p 1, k 1, LC, p 6.

Row 21: P 5, RC, (p 1, k 1) twice, LC, p 5.

Row 23: P 4, RC, (p 1, k 1) three times, LC, p 4.

Row 25: P 3, RC, (p 1, k 1) four times, LC, p 3.

Row 27: P 2, RC, (p 1, k 1) five times, LC, p 2.

Row 28: K 2, p 2, (k 1, p 1) six times, p 2, k 2. Repeat rows 3–28 for pat 4.

Note: Berries are embroidered in French knots after afghan is knitted.

AFGHAN:

With smaller needles, cast on 240 sts. Work in garter st for 1″. Change to larger needles.

Row 1 (right side): K 5, pat 1 on 15 sts, pat 2 on 10 sts, pat 3 on 20 sts, pat 2 on 10 sts; following chart, k from A to B, pat 2 on 10 sts, pat 1 on 20 sts, pat 4 on 20 sts, pat 1 on 20 sts, pat 2 on 10 sts; following chart, k from B to A, pat 2 on 10 sts, pat 3 on 20 sts, pat 2 on 10 sts, pat 1 on 15 sts, k 5.

Row 2: K 5, pat 1 on 15 sts, pat 2 on 10 sts, pat 3 on 20 sts, pat 2 on 10 sts; following chart, p from A to B, pat 2 on 10 sts, pat 1 on 20 sts, pat 4 on 20 sts, pat 1 on 20 sts, pat 2 on 10 sts, following chart, p from B to A, pat 2 on 10 sts, pat 3 on 20 sts, pat 2 on 10 sts, pat 1 on 15 sts, k 5. Continue as established until chart has been repeated thirteen times. Change to smaller needles. Work in garter st for 1″. With larger needles, bind off.

FINISHING:

With tapestry needle and C, work 3 French knots at center of each holly leaf motif.

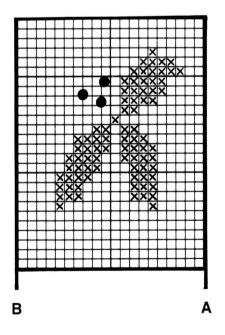

B   A

COLOR KEY

□ A

☒ B

● C

149

POINSETTIA BEDSPREAD

Rings of bright-red flowers on snow-white hexagons light up this gorgeous crocheted bedspread. Plain white motifs may be added around the edges to accommodate a larger-sized bed.

For how-to information, see Afghan Basics at the back of the book.

SIZE:
60" × 80", plus fringe

MATERIALS:
Worsted-weight, 4-ply yarn: 80 oz. White; 12 oz. Green; 8 oz. Red; and 4 oz. Yellow. Crochet hook size G (4.25 mm), or size required to obtain correct gauge.

GAUGE:
4 sts = 1". Motif is 6" from one side to opposite side.

BEDSPREAD:

POINSETTIA MOTIF (make 78): With Yellow, ch 4, join with sl st to form ring.

Rnd 1: Ch 3 (counts as 1 dc), 11 dc in ring. Sl st in top of ch 3. Cut yarn.

Rnd 2: Join Red in any dc, ch 8, * sc in 2nd ch from hook, hdc in next ch, dc in next 2 ch, hdc in next ch, sc in next ch, sc in next dc, ch 7, repeat from * ten times, sc in 2nd ch from hook, hdc in next ch, dc in next 2 ch, hdc in next ch, sc in last ch, sl st in first ch of first petal. Cut yarn.

Rnd 3: Join Green in any sc between petals; ch 5; * working in back of petals, dc in next sc between petals, ch 2, repeat from * around, sl st in 3rd ch of ch 5.

Rnd 4: Ch 9, * sc in 2nd ch from hook, hdc in next ch, dc in next ch, tr in next ch, dc in next ch, hdc in next ch, sc in next ch, 2 sc in ch-2 sp, sc in dc, ch 8, repeat from * ten times, work last ch 8 as before, 2 sc in ch-2 sp, sl st in first ch of first leaf. Cut yarn.

ASSEMBLY CHART

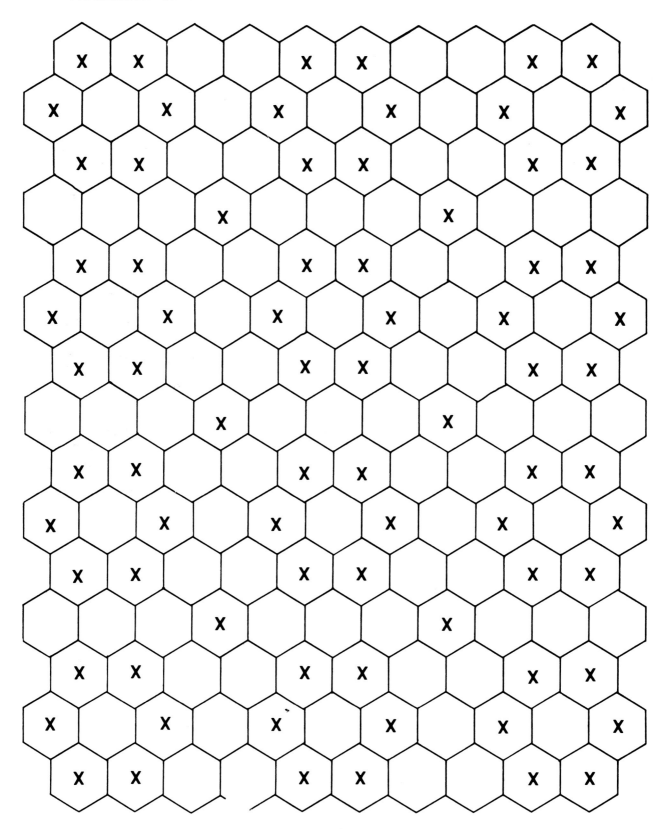

Rnd 5: With White, sc in each of 3 sc between leaves, * ch 1; working behind leaves, sc in each of next 3 sc, repeat from * around, end ch 1, sl st in first sc.

Rnd 6: Ch 1, sc in first sc, sc in next sc, * insert hook in sc at tip of red petal and into next sc of rnd 5 at same time, draw yarn through, complete sc, 2 sc in next ch-1 sp, sc in each of next 2 sc, repeat from * around, end 2 sc in last ch-1 sp, sl st in first sc.

Rnd 7: Ch 3 (counts as 1 dc), dc in each of next 3 sc, * ch 2, sk 1 sc, dc in each of next 4 sc, repeat from * around, end ch 2, sl st in top of ch 3.

Rnd 8: Ch 3, dc in each of next 3 dc, * dc in ch-2 sp, sc in sc at tip of leaf, dc in each of next 4 dc, repeat from * around, end dc in ch-2 sp, sc in tip of last leaf, sl st in top of ch 3.

Rnd 9: Ch 1, sc in each of first 5 dc, * sc in sc at tip of leaf, sc in each of next 2 dc, 3 dc in next dc (corner), sc in each of next 2 dc, sc in sc at tip of leaf, sc in each of next 5 dc, repeat from * around (6 corners), end sc in each of last 2 dc, sc in sc at tip of leaf, sl st in first sc. End off.

PLAIN MOTIF (make 79): With White, ch 4, join with sl st to form ring.

Rnd 1: Ch 3, 11 dc in ring, sl st in top of ch 3—12 dc.

Rnd 2: Ch 3, dc in same st, 2 dc in each dc around, sl st in top of ch 3—24 dc.

Rnd 3: Repeat rnd 2—48 dc.

Rnd 4: Ch 3, dc in each of next 3 dc, * ch 1, dc in each of next 4 dc, repeat from * around, ch 1, sl st in top of ch 3—12 ch-1 sps.

Rnd 5: Ch 3, dc in each of next 3 dc, * ch 2, dc in each of next 4 dc, repeat from * around, ch 2, sl st in top of ch 3—12 ch-1 sps.

Rnd 6: Ch 3, dc in each of next 3 dc, * 2 dc in ch-2 sp, dc in each of next 4 dc, repeat from * around, 2 dc in last sp, sl st in top of ch 3—72 dc.

Rnd 7: Ch 1, sc in same st, sc in next 7 dc, * 3 dc in next dc, sc in next 11 dc, repeat from * 4 times, sc in each of remaining 3 dc. Sl st in first sc. End off.

FINISHING:

Following chart, sew or sl st motifs tog to form bedspread, picking up back lps of sts only. When all motifs are joined, sc around entire bedspread with White.

FRINGE: Cut White in 6″ lengths. Knot one strand in each sc around edge.

WINTER WONDERLAND

For an exquisite coverlet that is extra-warm and reversible, try this double-knitting pattern. Winter motifs—in blue on one side, white on the other—are worked from a chart.

For how-to information, see Afghan Basics at the back of the book.

SIZE:
50" × 64"

MATERIALS:
Worsted-weight, 4-ply yarn: 28 oz. Cornflower Blue (B); 28 oz. White (W). Circular knitting needles, 29" long, No. 10 (6.5 mm), or size required to obtain correct gauge.

GAUGE:
20 sts = 3" (10 sts each side); 9 rows = 2".

DOUBLE KNITTING TECHNIQUE:
This technique, worked with two colors, produces a double thickness of knitting. One color predominates on one side, with the other color forming the pattern. Before working the afghan, make a swatch to practice double knitting, first without a design, then with a design.

With main color, cast on an even number of stitches.

Row 1 (right side): Join contrasting color to main color with a slip loop. * With both strands at back of work, k 1 main color; bring both strands to front of work, p 1 contrasting color. Repeat from * across. Twist strands tog at end of row to make a firm edge.

Row 2 (wrong side): * With both strands at back of work, k 1 contrasting color; bring both strands to front of work, p 1 main color. Repeat from * across.

Repeat right-side row and wrong-side row alternately for double knitting, always knitting the k sts and purling the p sts with the color of the stitch.

When working the design, k the design color on the right side and p the next st in the opposite color. Each row of chart represents one row of double knitting. Read the chart from right to left on right side, from left to right on wrong side.

AFGHAN:
With B, cast on 330 sts.

Row 1 (right side): Join W. * With both strands in back, k 1 B; with both strands in front, p 1 W; repeat from * across, end p 1 W.

Row 2 (wrong side): * With both strands in back, k 1 W; with both strands in front, p 1 B; repeat from * across, end p 1 B.

Row 3: Repeat row 1.

Working from chart, beg with row 4, work in pattern to top of chart. On right side (odd-numbered rows), Blue (B) is background color and White (W) is design color. On wrong side (even-numbered rows), White is background color and Blue is design color. Check both sides frequently to be sure you are using the correct color.

When top of chart is reached, turn chart upside down and work back to border. Do not repeat first row (center of afghan). When chart is complete, bind off with B, knitting the k sts and purling the p sts.

LUMBERJACK PLAID WITH POLAR BEARS

Bring a bit of the pine-scented North Woods into your home with this "lumberjack" plaid adapted for knitters. Polar bears and pines for the borders are worked later, using duplicate stitch.

For how-to information, see Afghan Basics at the back of the book.

SIZE:
52″ × 70″

MATERIALS:
Worsted-weight brushed acrylic yarn (such as Unger's Fluffy): 31½ oz. Black (A), 19¼ oz. Red (B); 1¾ oz. each White and Bright Green. Knitting needles No. 10 (6 mm), or size required to obtain correct gauge. Crochet hook size H (5 mm). Large-eyed tapestry needle.

GAUGE:
13 sts = 4″; 13 rows = 3″ (double strand).

PATTERN STITCH:

STOCKINETTE STITCH:
Row 1: Knit.
Row 2: Purl. Repeat rows 1 and 2 for stockinette stitch.

AFGHAN:
Use yarn doubled throughout afghan.

PANELS 1 and 3: With double strand of A, cast on 48 sts. Cut 1 strand of A, join 1 strand of B.
Row 1: With A and B, k 16; with 2 strands of A, k 16; with 1 strand each of A and B, k 16.
Row 2: With A and B, p 16; with 2 strands of A, p 16; with A and B, p 16.

COLOR KEY

◉ White
☒ Green

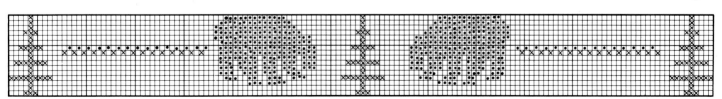

Rows 3–18: Continue in stockinette st with colors as established, twisting strands tog at color changes to avoid holes.

Rows 19–36: Continue in stockinette st, working 16 sts in B, 16 sts in A and B, 16 sts in B. Repeat these 36 rows six times, then rows 1–18 once—15 blocks. Bind off.

PANEL 2: With double strand of A, cast on 48 sts.

Row 1: With A, k 16; with A and B, k 16; with A, k 16.

Rows 2–18: Continue in stockinette st with colors as established.

Rows 19–36: With A and B, work 16 sts; with B, work 16 sts; with A and B, work 16 sts. Repeat these 36 rows six times, then rows 1–18 once—15 blocks. Bind off.

With A, sew panels tog.

BORDER: TOP and BOTTOM: From right side, with 2 strands of A, pick up and k 141 sts across top edge of afghan (47 sts across each panel). Work in stockinette st for 21 rows, inc 1 st each end every k row ten times—161 sts. Bind off.

SIDES: From right side, with 2 strands of A, pick up and k 225 sts along side edge of afghan (about 15 sts to each block). Work as for top border, including incs. Sew corner seams.

FINISHING:

With 2 strands of A, work 2 rows of sc around afghan, working 3 sc in each corner at each rnd.

EMBROIDERY: Referring to chart and color key and using 2 strands of yarn in needle, work polar bear and tree design on each side of border in duplicate st, centering design.

SNOWFIRE

A sensational pattern of white lacy "snowflakes" framed in flame-red squares of solid crochet. This afghan is certain to warm both the toes and the heart.

For how-to information, see Afghan Basics at the back of the book.

SIZE:
54" × 73"

MATERIALS:
Worsted-weight, 4-ply yarn: 36 oz. Red; 32 oz. white. Crochet hook size G (4.5 mm), or size required to obtain correct gauge.

GAUGE:
One square = 7¼".

AFGHAN:

SQUARE (make 70): With White, ch 6, sl st in first ch to form ring.

Rnd 1: Ch 3, 15 dc in ring. Join with sl st in top of ch-3.

Rnd 2: Ch 5, dc in same place as sl st, * sk next dc, work (dc, ch 2, dc) in next dc, repeat from * six times, sk last dc, join in 3rd ch of ch-5.

Rnd 3: Sl st in next ch-2 sp, (ch 3, dc, ch 3, 2 dc) in same sp, * (2 dc, ch 3, 2 dc) in next ch-2 sp, repeat from * six times, join in top of ch-3.

Rnd 4: Sl st to next ch-3 sp (ch 3, 2 dc, ch 3, 3 dc) in same sp, * (3 dc, ch 3, 3 dc) in next sp, repeat from * six times, join.

Rnd 5: Sl st across to ch-3 sp, (ch 3, 3 dc, ch 2, 4 dc) in same sp, * (4 dc, ch 2, 4 dc) in next sp, repeat from * six times, join. End off.

Rnd 6: Join Red with sl st in any ch-2 sp. (**Note:** For this rnd only, work in sps between dc's, not in the dc's.) * Sc in next sp, hdc in next sp, dc in each of next 5 sps, (2 dc, ch 2, 2 dc) in next ch-2 sp (corner); dc in each of next 5 sps, hdc in next sp, sc in next sp, sl st in next ch-2 sp, repeat from * three times, working last sl st in first sl st or rnd.

Rnd 7: Ch 1, sc in next sc, sc in next hdc, sc in next dc, * dc in each of next 6 dc, (2 dc, ch 3, 2 dc) in corner sp, dc in each of next 6 dc, sc in each of next dc, hdc, sc, sl st, sc, hdc, and dc, repeat from * three times, end last repeat sc in last 3 sts, sl st in ch 1 at beg of rnd.

Rnd 8: Ch 1, sc in each st around, working 3 sc in each corner sp, join with a sl st to ch 1 at beg of rnd. End off. Weave in all loose ends. Place square right-side-down on padded surface; lightly steampress so that square lies flat.

JOINING: Place two squares with right sides tog; join Red in upper righthand corner with a sl st through center sc in corner sps of both squares; join by working sl st loosely in back lps only across squares, carefully matching sts, end sl st in center sc in left-hand corner sp.

In same way, join 8 more squares into a strip 10 squares long. Make 7 strips of 10 squares each. Join strips lengthwise in same way.

FINISHING:

From right side, join Red with sc in back lp of center sc at upper right-hand corner, 2 sc more in same st, sc in back lp of each st around, working 3 sc in center st at each corner. Join to first sc. Place afghan right-side-down on padded surface; lightly steam-press each joining and outer edges.

Back Loops

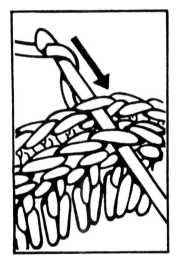

SNOW CRYSTALS

In this Scandinavian-style knit, the blue snowflakes are knitted directly into their frosty-white background. If you like, work the pattern in reverse—white flakes on a dark field.

For how-to information, see Afghan Basics at the back of the book.

SIZE:
45″ × 59″, plus fringe

MATERIALS:
Worsted-weight, 4-ply yarn: 24 oz. White; 20 oz. Navy. Knitting needles No. 9 (5.5 mm), or size required to obtain correct gauge. Stitch holders. Tapestry needle.

GAUGE:
4½ sts = 1″; 6 rows = 1″ (stockinette st).

PATTERN STITCHES:

STOCKINETTE STITCH:
Row 1: Knit.
Row 2: Purl. Repeat rows 1 and 2 for stockinette st.

MOSS STITCH: **Row 1:** K 1, * p 1, k 1, repeat from * across. Repeat row 1, always having a k st over a p st.

WEAVING TECHNIQUE: While knitting or purling, hold the contrasting yarn in the left hand. With each stitch, raise or lower the yarn so it can be caught in the stitch being worked, without showing from the right side.

AFGHAN:
With White, cast on 191 sts.
Row 1 (wrong side): Purl.
Row 2 (right side): K 43; pick up a strand of Navy and k 1; with White, k 103; with another strand of Navy, k 1; with White, k 43 (row 1 of chart). Continue to follow chart, working from A to B and from B to A (work center st once only). Change colors when necessary, weaving colors together as described above to prevent loose strands on the wrong side. When top of chart is reached, bind off.

BORDER: **Bottom:** With Navy, cast on 203 sts. Work in moss st for 6 rows.
Next Row (right side): (K 1, p 1) three times, put these 6 sts on a holder, bind off center 191 sts, (p 1, k 1) three times.
Side: Row 1: (K 1, p 1) three times.
Row 2: (P 1, k 1) three times. Repeat these 2 rows for a total of 348 rows; put these 6 sts on a holder and set aside.

With another ball of Navy, pick up the sts from the first holder and work in moss st until the same measurement as the first side (348 rows total).
Top: (K 1, p 1) three times, cast on 191 sts, (p 1, k 1) three times. Work in moss st for 6 rows; bind off.

FINISHING:

Sew or weave bottom, top, and sides
to afghan, stitch for stitch. Weave
in ends. Steam-press if necessary.

FRINGE: Cut Navy in 18″ strands.
Using 4 strands for each fringe,
knot fringe in every 3rd st across top
and bottom of afghan.

COLOR KEY ☐ White
☒ Navy

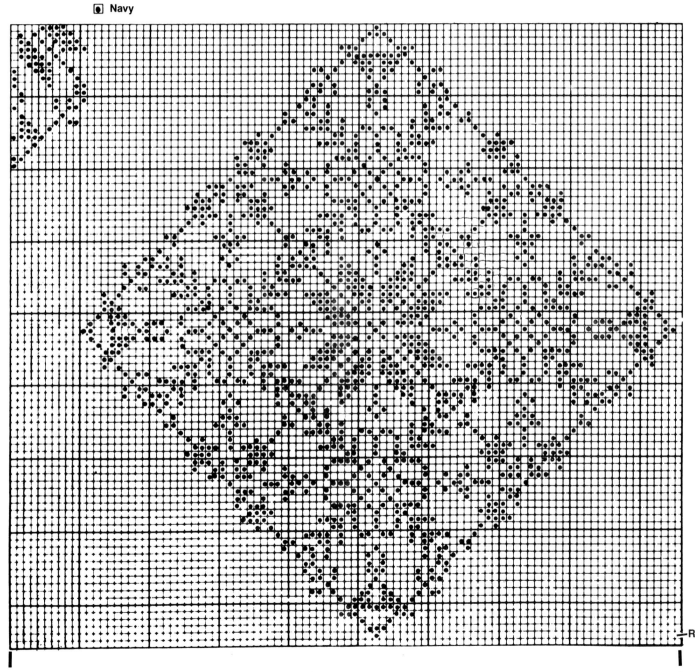

B   A

B   A

COLOR KEY ☐ White
◉ Navy

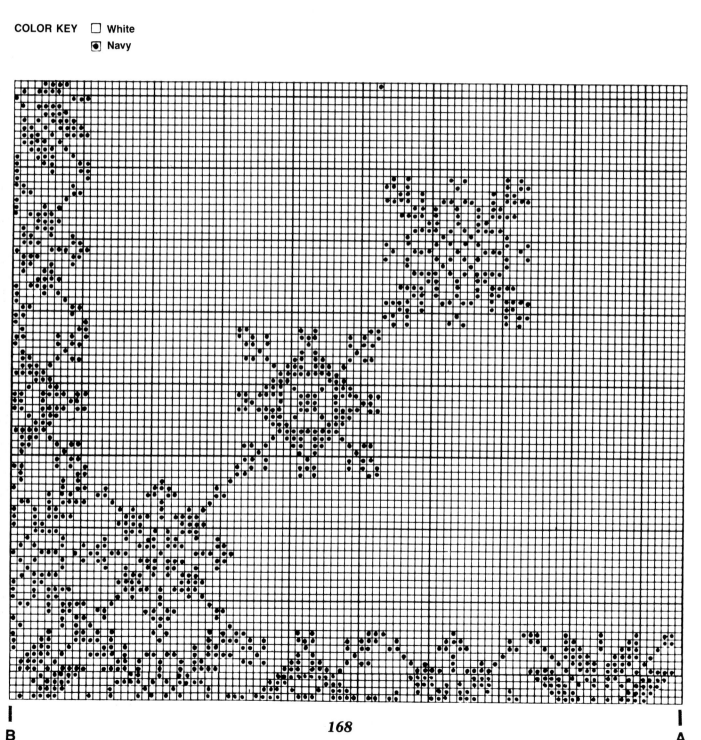

B

A

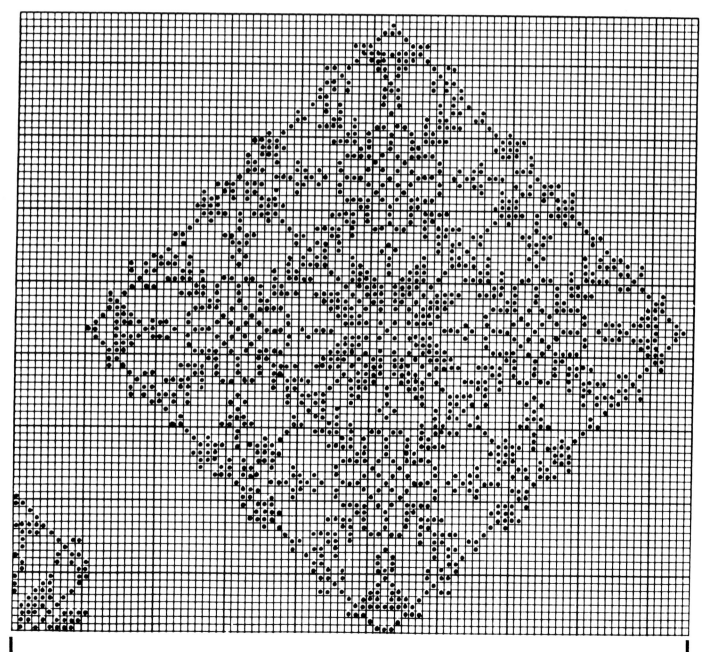

B

A

CRISSCROSS CROCHET

Dramatic stitchery holds center stage in this imaginative crochet. Cables are crisscrossed to create an all-over pattern of diamonds. A lovely crisscrossed border of lattice weaving continues the theme, and edges are rounded off with shell stitch.

For how-to information, see Afghan Basics at the back of the book.

SIZE:
57″ × 65″

MATERIALS:
Sport-weight yarn: 52½ oz. Blue. Crochet hook size K (6.5 mm), or size required to obtain correct gauge.

GAUGE:
16 sts = 4″

SPECIAL ABBREVIATIONS:
Bpdc: Back post double crochet: Yo, insert hook from back to front to back around post of next st, yo and pull up a lp, (yo and pull through 2 lps on hook) twice.

Fpdc: Front post double crochet: Yo, insert hook from front to back to front around post of next st, yo and pull up a lp, (yo and pull through 2 lps on hook) twice.

FC: Front cross: Sk 3 sts, fpdc in each of next 3 sts, bring hook in front of sts just made and fpdc in each skipped st—front cross on 6 sts.

BC: Back cross: Sk 3 sts, bpdc in each of next 3 sts, bring hook behind sts just made and bpdc in each skipped st—back cross on 6 sts.

Flt: Front left twist: Sk 1 st, bpdc in each of next 2 sts, bring hook in front of sts just made and fpdc in skipped st—front left twist on 3 sts.

Frt: Front right twist: Sk 2 sts, fpdc in next st, bring hook behind st just made and bpdc in each skipped st—front right twist on 3 sts.

Blt: Back left twist: Sk 2 sts, bpdc in next st, bring hook in front of st just made and fpdc in each skipped st—back left twist on 3 sts.

Brt: Back right twist: Sk 1 st, fpdc in each of next 2 sts, bring hook behind st just made and bpdc in skipped st—back right twist on 3 sts.

AFGHAN:
Note: Ch 2, turn each row (ch-2 does not count as a st).

Ch 186. Dc in 3rd ch from hook and in each ch across—184 dc.

Row 1 (right side): Fpdc, * 4 bpdc, FC, 4 bpdc, repeat from * across, end fpdc.

Row 2: Bpdc, * 4 fpdc, 6 bpdc, 4 fpdc, repeat from * across, end bpdc.

Row 3: Fpdc, * 2 bpdc, frt, 4 fpdc, flt, 2 bpdc, repeat from * across, end fpdc.

Row 4: Bpdc, * blt, 2 fpdc, 4 bpdc, 2 fpdc, brt, repeat from * across, end bpdc.

Row 5: Fpdc, * fpdc, 2 bpdc, frt, 2 fpdc, flt, 2 bpdc, fpdc, repeat from * across, end fpdc.

Row 6: Bpdc, * bpdc, blt, 2 fpdc, 2 bpdc, 2 fpdc, brt, bpdc, repeat from * across, end bpdc.

Row 7: Fpdc, * 2 fpdc, 2 bpdc, frt, flt, 2 bpdc, 2 fpdc, repeat from * across, end fpdc.

Row 8: Bpdc, * 2 bpdc, blt, 4 fpdc, brt, 2 bpdc, repeat from * across, end bpdc.

Rows 9 and 11: Fpdc, * 3 fpdc, 8 bpdc, 3 fpdc, repeat from * across, end fpdc.

Row 10: 4 bpdc, 8 fpdc, * BC, 8 fpdc, repeat from * across, end 4 bpdc.

Row 12: Bpdc, * 2 bpdc, brt, 4 fpdc, blt, 2 bpdc, repeat from * across, end bpdc.

Row 13: Fpdc, * 2 fpdc, 2 bpdc, flt, frt, 2 bpdc, 2 fpdc, repeat from * across, end fpdc.

Row 14: Bpdc, * bpdc, brt, 2 fpdc, 2 bpdc, 2 fpdc, blt, bpdc, repeat from * across, end bpdc.

Row 15: Fpdc, * fpdc, 2 bpdc, flt, 2 fpdc, frt, 2 bpdc, fpdc, repeat from * across, end fpdc.

Row 16: Bpdc, * brt, 2 fpdc, 4 bpdc, 2 fpdc, blt, repeat from * across, end bpdc.

Row 17: Fpdc, * 2 bpdc, flt, 4 fpdc, frt, 2 bpdc, repeat from * across, end fpdc.

Row 18: Repeat row 2. Repeat rows 1–18 for pat. Work until piece measures about 60″ from beg, end pat row 2 or 11.

BORDER: From right side, beg at top right corner, work the following rnds, making 2 sts in each of 2 corner sts for incs.

Rnd 1: Working along side edge, pick up fpdc edge st, inc at corner, * ch 1, sk 1 st, dc in next st, bring hook in front of st just made and dc in skipped st, repeat from * across, inc at corner, working along first row, ** ch 1, sk 2 sts, fpdc in next st, bring hook in front of st just made and fpdc in st before one just made **, repeat from ** to ** across, inc at corner, repeat from * to * along other side edge, inc at corner, repeat from ** to ** along last row; sl st in first st to join each rnd.

Rnd 2: Inc at corner, * ch 1, sk 1 st, bpdc in next bpdc, bring hook behind st just made and bpdc in skipped bpdc, repeat from * around inc, at corner.

Rnd 3: Inc at corner, * ch 1, sk 1 st, fpdc in next fpdc, bring hook in front of st just made and fpdc in skipped fpdc, repeat from * around, inc at corner. Repeat rnds 2 and 3 until 6 rnds have been completed; ch 1 at end of last rnd.

Shell Rnd: * Sc in next ch-1 sp, (dc, ch 1, dc, ch 1, dc) in next ch-1 sp, repeat from * around. End off.

AFGHAN BASICS

- **Crochet**
- **Afghan Stitch**
- **Knitting**
- **Embroidery Stitches**
- **General Directions for Crocheters and Knitters**

CROCHET

CROCHET ABBREVIATIONS

ch—chain stitch
st—stitch
sts—stitches
lp—loop
inc—increase
dec—decrease
rnd—round
beg—beginning
sk—skip
p—picot
tog—together
lp—loop

sc—single crochet
sl st—slip stitch
dc—double crochet
hdc—half double crochet
tr—treble or triple crochet
dtr—double treble crochet
tr tr—treble treble crochet
bl—block
sp—space
cl—cluster
pat—pattern
yo—yarn over hook

HOW TO FOLLOW DIRECTIONS:

An asterisk (*) is often used in crochet directions to indicate repetition. For example, when directions read "* 2 dc in next st, 1 dc in next st, repeat from * four times" this means to work directions after first * four times more. Work five times in all.

When parentheses ( ) are used to show repetition, work directions within parentheses as many times as specified. For example, "(dc, ch 1) three times" means to do what is within ( ) three times altogether.

"Work even" in directions means to work in the same pattern stitch on the same number of stitches, without increasing or decreasing.

CHAIN STITCH

To make first loop on hook, grasp yarn about 2 inches from end between left thumb and index finger. With right hand, lap long strand over short end, forming a loop. Hold loop in place with left thumb and index finger.

Fig. 1

Figure 1: Grasp hook in right hand, insert hook through loop, catch strand with hook and draw it through loop. Pull end and long strand in opposite directions to close loop around hook.

Drawing the yarn through the loop on the hook makes this chain stitch. Repeat step until you have as many chains as you need. One loop always remains on hook. Practice making all chains uniform.

Fig. 2

Figure 2: Weave yarn through left hand.

SINGLE CROCHET

Fig. 1

Figure 1: Insert hook in second chain from hook. Yarn over hook.

Fig. 2

Figure 2: Draw yarn through chain—2 loops on hook.

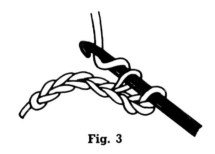

Fig. 3

Figure 3: Yarn over hook. Draw yarn through 2 loops on hook. One single crochet has been made.

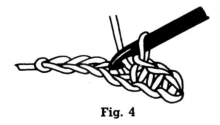

Fig. 4

Figure 4: Work a single crochet in each chain stitch. At end of row, chain 1 and turn work around.

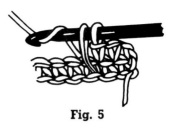

Fig. 5

Figure 5: Insert hook under both top loops of stitch below, yarn over hook and draw through stitch. Yarn over and through 2 loops on hook. Work a single crochet in same way in each stitch across row.

Fig. 6

Figure 6: To make a ridge stitch or slipper stitch, work rows of single crochet by inserting hook in back loop only of each single crochet.

HOW TO INCREASE 1 SINGLE CROCHET

Work 2 stitches in 1 stitch.

HOW TO DECREASE 1 SINGLE CROCHET

Pull up a loop in 1 stitch, pull up a loop in next stitch (3 loops on hook), yarn over hook, draw through all 3 loops at once.

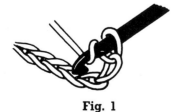

SLIP STITCH

Insert hook in work. Yarn over hook and draw through both the stitch and the loop on hook. Slip stitch makes a firm finishing edge. A single slip stitch is used for joining a chain to form a ring.

HALF-DOUBLE CROCHET

Fig. 1

Figure 1: Yarn over hook. Insert hook in third chain from hook.

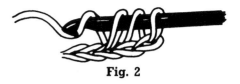

Fig. 2

Figure 2: Yarn over hook, draw through chain. Yarn over hook again.

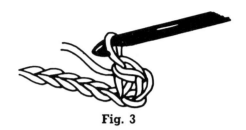

Fig. 3

Figure 3: Draw through all 3 loops on hook. One half-double crochet has been made.

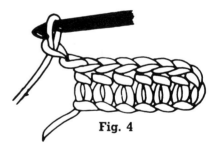

Fig. 4

Figure 4: Work a half-double crochet in each chain across. At end of row, chain 2 and turn work.

DOUBLE CROCHET

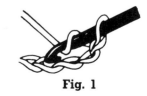

Fig. 1

Figure 1: Yarn over hook. Insert hook in fourth chain from hook.

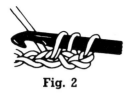

Fig. 2

Figure 2: Yarn over hook. Draw through chain. There are 3 loops on hook.

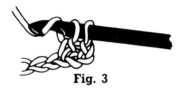

Fig. 3

Figure 3: Yarn over hook. Draw through 2 loops on hook. There are 2 loops on hook. Yarn over hook.

Fig. 4

Figure 4: Draw yarn through remaining 2 loops on hook. One double crochet has been made. When you have worked a double crochet in each chain across, chain 3 and turn work. In most directions, the turning chain-3 counts as first double crochet of next row. In working the second row, skip the first stitch and work a double crochet in the 2 top loops of each double crochet across. The last double crochet of each row is worked in the top chain of the chain-3 turning chain.

TREBLE or TRIPLE CROCHET (tr)

With 1 loop on hook put yarn over hook twice, insert in fifth chain from hook, pull loop through. Yarn over and draw through 2 loops at a time three times. At end of a row, chain 4 and turn. Chain-4 counts as first treble of next row.

DOUBLE TREBLE (dtr)

Put yarn over hook three times and work off 2 loops at a time as for treble.

TREBLE TREBLE (tr tr)

Put yarn over hook four times and work off 2 loops at a time as for treble.

AFGHAN STITCH

PLAIN AFGHAN STITCH

Work with afghan hook. Make a ch desired length.

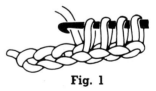

Fig. 1

Figure 1: Row 1: Keeping all loops on hook, skip first chain from hook (loop on hook is first stitch), pull up a loop in each chain across.

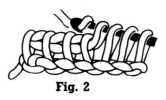

Fig. 2

Figure 2: To Work Lps Off: Yarn over hook, pull through first loop, * yarn over hook, pull through next 2 loops, repeat from * across until 1 loop remains. Loop that remains on hook always counts as first stitch of next row.

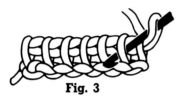

Fig. 3

Figure 3: Row 2: Keeping all loops on hook, skip first vertical bar (loop on hook is first stitch), pull up a loop under next vertical bar and under each vertical bar across. Work loops off as before. Repeat row 2 for plain afghan stitch.

Edge Stitch: Made at end of rows only to make a firm edge. Work as follows: Insert hook under last vertical bar and in loop at back of bar, pull up 1 loop.

HALF CROSS-STITCH ON AFGHAN STITCH

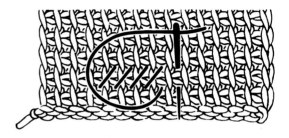

CROSS-STITCH ON AFGHAN STITCH

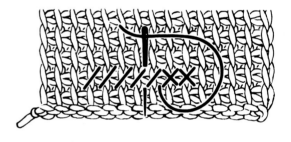

HOW TO TURN YOUR WORK

In crochet a certain number of ch sts are needed at the end of each row to bring work into position for the next row. Then the work is turned so reverse side is facing the crocheter. Follow the stitch table below for the number of ch sts to make a turn.

Single crochet (sc)	Ch 1 to turn
Half-double crochet (half dc or hdc)	Ch 2 to turn
Double crochet (dc)	Ch 3 to turn
Treble crochet (tr)	Ch 4 to turn
Double treble crochet (dtr)	Ch 5 to turn
Treble treble crochet (tr tr)	Ch 6 to turn

KNITTING

KNITTING ABBREVIATIONS

k—knit	**psso**—pass slip stitch over
p—purl	**inc**—increase
st—stitch	**dec**—decrease
sts—stitches	**beg**—beginning
yo—yarn over	**pat**—pattern
sl—slip	**lp**—loop
sk—skip	**MC**—main color
tog—together	**CC**—contrasting color
rnd—round	**dp**—double-pointed

HOW TO FOLLOW DIRECTIONS

The asterisk (*) is used in directions to mark the beginning and end of any part of the directions that is to be repeated one or more times. For example, "* k 9, p 3, repeat from * four times" means to work directions after first * until second * is reached, then go back to first * four times more. Work five times in all.

When parentheses ( ) are used to show repetition, work directions in parentheses as many times as specified. For example "(k 9, p 3) four times" means to do what is in ( ) four times altogether.

CASTING ON

There are many ways of casting on stitches. The method shown here is only one of them. It gives you a strong and elastic edge.

Fig. 1

Figure 1: Allow enough yarn for the number of stitches to be cast on (about ½ inch per stitch for light weight yarns such as baby yarns, 1 inch per stitch for heavier yarns such as knitting worsted, more for bulky yarns on large needles). Make a slip loop on needle and tighten knot gently.

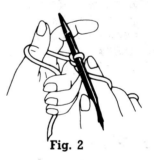

Fig. 2

Figure 2: Hold needle in right hand with short end of yarn over left thumb. Weave strand that comes from ball through right hand, over index finger, under second, over third and under fourth finger.

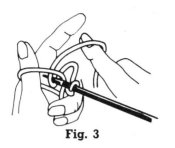

Fig. 3

Figure 3: Bring needle forward to make a loop over left thumb. Insert needle from left to right in loop; bring yarn in right hand under, then over point of needle and draw yarn through loop with tip of needle.

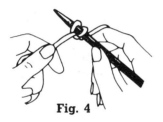

Fig. 4

Figure 4: Keeping right hand in same position, tighten stitch on needle gently with left hand. You now have 2 stitches on needle. Repeat Figures 3 and 4 for required number of stitches.

KNIT STITCH

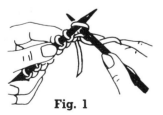

Fig. 1

Figure 1: Hold needle with cast-on stitches in left hand and yarn in same position as for casting on in right hand. Insert point of needle from left to right in first stitch.

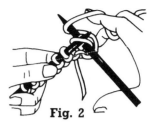

Fig. 2

Figure 2: Bring yarn under and over point of right needle.

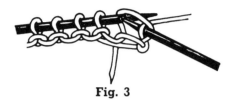

Fig. 3

Figure 3: Draw yarn through stitch with point of needle.

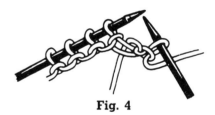

Fig. 4

Figure 4: Allow loop on left needle to slip off needle. Loop on right needle is your first knit stitch. Repeat from Figure 1 in each loop across row. When you have finished knitting one row, place needle with stitches in left hand ready to start next row.

GARTER STITCH

If you work row after row of knit stitch, you are working garter stitch.

180

PURL STITCH

To purl, insert needle from right to left in stitch on left needle. Bring yarn over and under point of right needle: Draw yarn back through stitch and allow loop on left needle to slip off needle.

STOCKINETTE STITCH

If you work one row of knit stitch and one row of purl stitch alternately, you are working stockinette stitch.

Stockinette Stitch

Knit Side

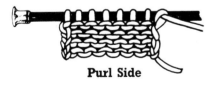

Purl Side

REVERSE STOCKINETTE STITCH

If you work one row of purl stitch and one row of knit stitch alternately, you are working reverse stockinette stitch.

BINDING OFF

Knit the first 2 stitches. Insert left needle from left to right through front of first stitch. Lift first stitch over second stitch and over tip of right needle. One stitch has been bound off, 1 stitch remains on right needle. Knit another stitch. Again lift first stitch over second stitch and off right needle. Continue across until all stitches have been bound off. One loop remains on needle. Cut yarn, pull end through loop, and tighten knot.

TO INCREASE ONE STITCH

There are several ways to increase a stitch.

Method 1

Method 1 is illustrated. Knit 1 stitch in the usual way, but do not slip if off left needle. Bring right needle behind left needle, insert it from right to left in same stitch (called "the back of the stitch") and make another knit stitch. Slip stitch off left needle. To increase 1 stitch on the purl stitch, purl 1 stitch but do not slip it off left needle. Bring yarn between needles to back, knit 1 stitch in back of same stitch.
Method 2: Pick up horizontal strand between stitch just knitted and next stitch, place it on left needle.

Knit 1 stitch in back of this strand, thus twisting it.

Method 3: Place right needle behind left needle. Insert right needle in stitch below next stitch, knit this stitch, then knit stitch above it in the usual way.

TO DECREASE ONE STITCH

On the right side of work, knit 2 stitches together as shown through the front of the stitches (the decrease slants to the right), or through the back of the stitches (the decrease slants to the left). On the purl side, purl 2 stitches together.

Another decrease stitch is called "psso" (pass slip stitch over). When directions say "sl 1, k 1, psso," slip first stitch (take it from left to right needle without knitting it), knit next stitch, then bring slip stitch over knit stitch as in binding off.

DUPLICATE STITCH

This embroidery stitch looks the same as knitted-in designs and is worked after piece is knitted. Thread tapestry needle with yarn of contrasting color. Draw yarn from wrong side of work to right side

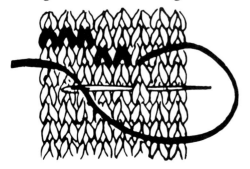

through center of lower point of stitch. Insert needle at top right-hand side of same stitch. Then, holding needle in horizontal position, draw through top left-hand side of stitch and insert again into base of stitch to left of where needle came out at start of stitch. Keep yarn loose enough to lie on top of work and cover knitted stitch.

TO CROCHET AN EDGE ON KNITTING

From right side and working from right to left, unless otherwise specified, work 1 sc in each stitch on bound-off or cast-on edges or sc in spaces along front or side edges; work 2 or 3 sc at corners to keep work flat. To attach yarn, insert hook into stitch or space. Draw yarn through, forming a loop, yarn over hook and through loop on hook, * insert hook into stitch or space on edge, draw yarn through, yarn over hook and through both loops on hook, repeat from * to end. End off by cutting yarn and pulling through loop on back.

CRAB STITCH (Reverse Crochet)

For a decorative finish, work reverse crochet: Either work one row sc from left to right or work one row sc from right to left, one row sc from left to right.

KNIT KNOW-HOW

Here are some more useful hints for knitters.

To Yarn Over When Knitting—Bring yarn under right needle to front, then over needle to back, ready to knit next stitch.

To Yarn Over When Purling—Bring yarn up over right needle to back, then under needle to front, ready to purl next stitch.

To Pick Up and Knit Stitches on Edges—Place new strand of yarn under edge. Working from right to left, use a crochet hook to * pick up a loop through knitted stitch in row below edge. Place loop around right-hand needle. Repeat from * until required number of stitches are picked up.

The number of stitches to be picked up for a sleeve is based on armhole length and stitch gauge. Since you will be knitting these stitches, it is essential that they be evenly spaced along edge. With care, stitches can be picked up by using a needle only.

To Slip a Stitch—Insert right needle into stitch as if to knit stitch (unless directions read "as if to purl") and then slip stitch from the left needle to the right needle without knitting or purling it.

To Change Yarn Color—When changing from one color to another, whether working on right or wrong side, pick up the new strand from under dropped strand.

To Ravel Stitches—When it is necessary to ravel work and then pick up the stitches again, it is advisable to rip last row stitch by stitch, placing each stitch (as if to purl) on a fine needle. Then work these stitches onto correct-sized needle.

To Pick Up a Dropped Stitch—Use a crochet hook. In stockinette stitch, insert hook through loop of dropped stitch from front to back of work, hook facing upward. * Pull horizontal thread of next row above stitch on hook through loop; repeat from * to top. Place stitch on needle. If pattern stitch is used, pick up stitch in pattern.

EMBROIDERY STITCHES

Cross-Stitch

French Knot

Chain Stitch

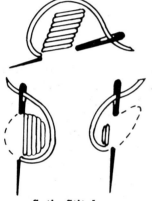

Satin Stitch

Outline Stitch

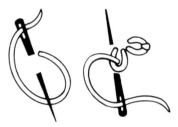

Lazy Daisy Stitch

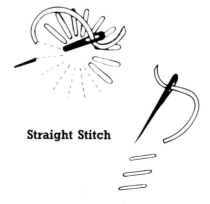

Straight Stitch

GENERAL DIRECTIONS FOR CROCHETERS AND KNITTERS

CROCHET HOOKS

CROCHET HOOKS (ALUMINUM OR PLASTIC)

U.S.	1/B	2/C	3/D	4/E	5/F	6/G	8/H	9/I	10/J	10½/K
English	12	11	10	9	8	7	6	5	4	2
Continental—mm	2.25	2.75	3.25	3.5	3.75	4.25	5	5.5	6	6.5

CROCHET HOOKS (STEEL)

U.S.	1	2	3	4	5	6	7	8	9	10	11	12	13	14
English	3/0	2/0	1/0	1	1½	2	2½	3	4	5	5½	6	6½	7
Continental—mm		3	2.5		2		1.75	1.5	1.25	1	0.75		0.6	

Crochet hooks come in a large range of sizes, from the very fine No. 14 steel hook for fine crochet cotton to larger hooks of aluminum or plastic for coarser cotton, wool, or other yarns.

STEEL CROCHET HOOKS

These are 5 inches long and come in size 00 (large) to 14 (very fine). Steel hooks are generally used for cotton threads, but the larger sizes are often used for other yarns.

PLASTIC AND ALUMINUM HOOKS

Plastic crochet hooks are 5 inches long and come in sizes B to K. These hooks sometimes carry a number, too. The numbers, however, are not standard.

"Bone" crochet hooks are 5 inches long and come in sizes 1 to 6, roughly the equivalent of B to G shown in illustration.

Aluminum crochet hooks are 6 inches long and come in sizes B to K.

Afghan hooks of aluminum and plastic are 9 inches to 18 inches long and have a straight, even shaft. They range from sizes 1 to 10½ and B to K. When afghan hooks are sized by number, the shaft of each hook is roughly equal to the same size in knitting needles. When they are sized by letter, they are equivalent to crochet hooks sized in the same way.

WOODEN CROCHET HOOKS

These are 9 inches or 10 inches long in sizes 10 to 16, and are used for jiffy work. For extra-bulky crochet, hollow plastic hooks are available in sizes Q and S.

KNITTING NEEDLES

U.S.	0	1	2	3	4	5	6	7	8	9	10	10½	11	13	15
English	13	12	11	10	9	8	7	6	5	4	3	2	1	00	000
Continental—mm	2	2.25	2.75	3.25	3.5	3.75	4.25	4.5	5	5.5	6	6.5	8	9	10

Single-pointed needles of aluminum, plastic, or wood are used in pairs to knit back and forth in rows. For ease in working, choose a color to contrast with the yarn. Colored aluminum and plastic needles come in 7-inch, 10-inch, and 14-inch lengths, in sizes varying from 1 to 5 in the shorter lengths and 1 to 10½, 11, 13, and 15 in the longer lengths. Colored aluminum needles also come in size 0. Wood needles, 14 inches long, come in sizes 11 to 15. Even larger sizes for jiffy knitting—17, 18, 19, 35, and 50—are available in hollow plastic. Flexible "jumper" needles of nylon or nylon and aluminum are available in 18-inch lengths in sizes 1 to 15.

Double-pointed (dp) needles are used in sets of four for tubular knitting for items as socks, mittens, gloves, and sleeves worked without seams. Of plastic or aluminum, they come in 5-inch, 7-inch, and 10-inch lengths. Plastic double-pointed needles come in sizes 1 to 15, aluminum in 0 to 8.

Circular knitting needles of nylon come in 16-inch to 29-inch lengths in sizes 0 to 10½; the 29-inch length is also made in sizes 11, 13, and 15; a 35-inch length is made in sizes 5 to 15. Circular needles are used for knitting skirts without seams, circular yokes, and other tubular pieces, but may be used for knitting back and forth in flat knitting, too. They are especially useful for afghans and other large pieces that require a great many stitches.

ACCESSORIES

Many accessories are available to the knitter. *Stitch holders* keep one section of knitting from raveling while another section is being worked; *counters* keep track of increases, decreases, stitches, and rows; *needle point-guards* keep knitting on needles when not in use; *bobbins* or *snap yarn holder* are useful when knitting in small areas of color; little *ring markers* mark pattern sections; *needle gauges* determine the correct sizes of needles.

HOOKS AND NEEDLES

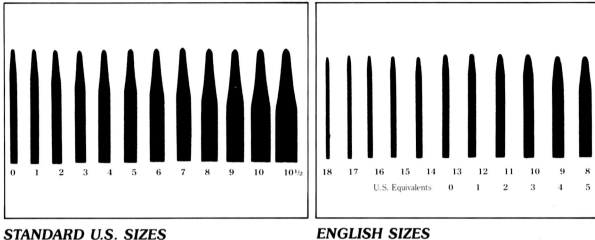

STANDARD U.S. SIZES   **ENGLISH SIZES**

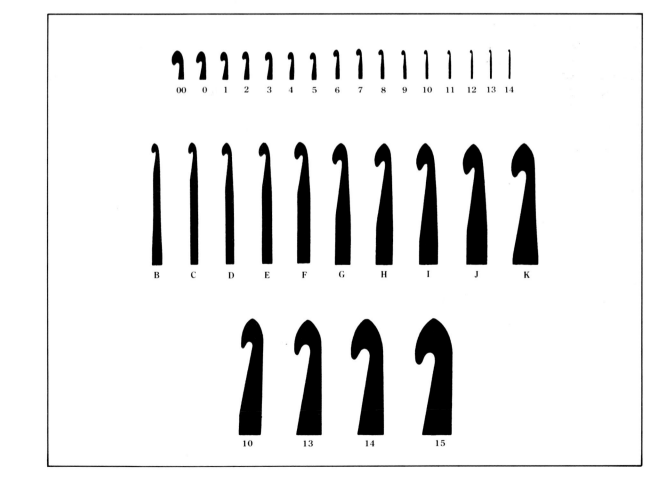

MEASURING YOUR GAUGE

Most knitting and crochet directions include a stitch gauge. The stitch gauge gives the number of stitches to the inch with the yarn and hook or needles recommended in the pattern stitch. The directions are based on the given gauge. The gauge (or tension) at which you work controls the size of each finished piece. It is therefore essential to work to the gauge given for each item if you want it to be the correct size. To test your gauge, cast on 20–30 stitches, using the hook or needles specified. Work in the pattern stitches for 3 inches. Smooth out your swatch and pin it down. Measure across 2 inches and place pins 2 inches apart. Count number of stitches between pins. If you have more stitches to the inch than directions specify, you are working too tightly; use a larger hook or needles and measure again. If you have fewer stitches to the inch, you are working too loosely; use a smaller hook or needles and measure again.

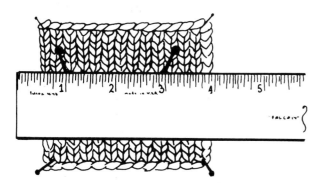

Most patterns give a row gauge, too. Although the proper length does not usually depend on the row gauge (directions usually give lengths in inches rather than rows), in some patterns it is important to have the proper row gauge, too.

TO ENLARGE A PATTERN

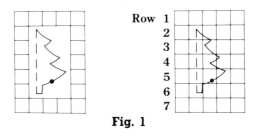

Fig. 1

Figure 1: Using ruler and sharp pencil, draw lines across pattern, connecting grid lines. Count number of boxes on grid both across and down.

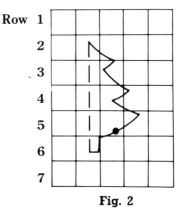

Fig. 2

Figure 2: On a large piece of paper, draw the same number of boxes, making sides of each box same size indicated on the pattern. For example, if the pattern says that one square on the grid equals 1 inch, make sides of each box 1 inch.

Begin at box in upper left corner of grid. On sample, there are no design lines in first box or in any other box in row 1. Move down to row 2 and note that first box is also blank. But in second box there is a straight line (part of long dash line) and a curved line which meet about one quarter down from top of box, about halfway between box sides. The straight line goes down to bottom of box, and the curved line goes to a point on right side of box about one third up from bottom. Draw lines that correspond with these lines on your piece of paper. Box by box, copy design lines and all markings (such as closed and open dots, letters, numbers, arrows, and so on) to look the same way on your paper as they do on original pattern.

HOW TO MAKE FRINGE

Cut strands of yarn double the length of fringe desired. Fold strands in half.

Fig. 1

Figure 1: Insert a crochet hook from front to back of edge where fringe is being made, and pull through the folded end of yarn strand.

Fig. 2

Figure 2: Insert the two ends through loop and pull ends to tighten fringe. Repeat across edge with each doubled strand, placing strands close together, or distance apart desired. For a fuller fringe, group a few strands together, and work as for one strand fringe.

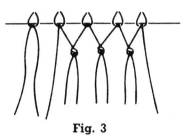

Fig. 3

Figure 3: The fringe may be knotted after all strands are in place along edge. To knot, separate the ends of two adjacent fringes (or divide grouped fringes in half); hold together the adjacent ends and knot 1 inch or more below edge. Hold second end with one end of next fringe and knot together the same distance below edge as first knot. Continue across in this manner. A second row of knots may be made by separating the knotted ends again and knotting together ends from two adjacent fringes in same manner as for first row of knots.

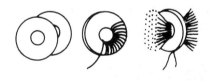

HOW TO MAKE POMPONS

Cut two cardboard disks desired size of pompon; cut ¼" hole in center of both. Thread needle with two strands of yarn. Place disks together; cover with yarn, working through holes. Slip scissors between disks; cut all strands at outside edge. Draw a long strand of yarn down between disks and wind several times very tightly around yarn; knot, leaving ends for attaching pompon. Remove cardboard disks and fluff out pompon.

BLOCKING

Lay pieces right-side-up on a flat, padded surface and straighten. Place rustproof pins at top and bottom corners of each piece, measuring to ensure correct length and width. Continue pinning all around outer edges, keeping patterns straight. Do not pin ribbings. Cover with damp cloth. Let dry. Do not press.

Mohair, fluffy yarns, and raised pattern stitches can be steamed: Hold iron just above pieces, as close as possible without touching, and move slowly over entire surface, making sure steam penetrates piece. If yarn is extra heavy, use a spray iron or wet pressing cloth.

When blocked pieces are dry, remove pins and sew together.

INDEX

A
abbreviations:
    crochet, 174
    knitting, 179
Add A Strip, 100
Afghan Basics, 173
afghan stitch, 177–178

B
Baby Granny, 131
Baby Rose, 133
Baby Quilt and Pillow, 136
back loops, 163
Basketweave Floral Coverlet, 14
binding off, knit, 181
blocking, 190
Blue Cables, 63
Blue Star "Quilt," 113
bobbles, 29
Brick-Washed Argyle, 77

C
Candy-Stripe Ribbons and Bows,
    baby blanket, 120;
    crib bumper covers, 122;
    pillow, 122
Carrousel Horses, 127
chain stitch, crochet, 174
chain stitch, embroidery, 184
Color-Chrome Narrow Steps, 105
Color-Chrome Wide Steps, 102
Colorglow, 84
Corner To Corner, 86
Country Casual, 73
Cozy Aran, 89
Cozy Bow Coverlet, 67
crab stitch, 182
Crayon Box, 143
Crisscross Crochet, 171
crochet, 174–178

crochet hooks, 185, 187
cross-stitch, 184
cross-stitch on afghan stitch, 178

D
decrease:
    crochet, 176
    knitting, 182
Designer Accents, 13
double crochet, 176–177
double treble, 177
duplicate stitch, 182

E
edge stitch, 178
embroidery stitches, 184
enlarge pattern, 188

F
Fanciful Flowers, 59
filet crochet, 136
Floral Cable, 69
Flower Baskets, 74
Flower Diamonds, 29
Folk-Art Tree, 79
French knot, 184
fringes, 189
From My Garden, 25

G
garter stitch, 180
gauge, 188
general directions, 185
Geranium, afghan and pillow, 37
Girls, Boys, Baby's Toys, 119
Golden Bells, 64

H
half cross-stitch on afghan stitch, 178

half-double crochet, 176
Harvest Glow, 49
Hats and Mittens, 123
Holly Aran, 148

I
increase:
    crochet, 175
    knitting, 181–182
Introduction, 9

K
knit know-how, 183
knit stitch, 180
knitting, 179–183
knitting accessories, 186
knitting needles, 186–187

L
Lacy and Luxurious, 53
lazy daisy stitch, 184
Log Cabin, 110
Lumberjack Plaid with Polar Bears, 159

M
Midnight Magic, 41

N
Nosegays For Spring, 33

O
Octagon Mosaic, 91
outline stitch, 184

P
Patterns with Pizazz, 99
Peach Fluff, 55
Picnic Plaid, 108

Pinwheels, 95
Plaid Coverlet, 19
plain afghan stitch, 177
Poinsettia Bedspread, 150
pompons, 189
popcorns, 29
purl stitch, 181

Q
Quick-Crochet Carriage Cover, 129
Quick-Crochet Granny, 82
Quilt Check, afghan, 44–45;
    square pillow, 46; oblong pillow, 47

R
Rose Petals with White Blossoms, 54
reverse stockinette stitch, 181

S
satin stitch, 184
single crochet, 175
slip stitch, 176
Snow Crystals, 165
Snowfire, 161
stockinette stitch, 181
straight stitch, 184
Sunset Ripple, 116
Sweet Dreams, blanket, 139; pillowtop, 140

T
treble crochet, 177
treble-treble crochet, 177
Tulip Patch, afghan, 21; pillow, 24
Two-Tone Check, 20

W
Warm and Wintry, 147
Winter Wonderland, 155